WRITING
RESEARCH
PAPERS

a
complete
guide

JAMES D. LESTER
Kansas State Teachers College

SCOTT, FORESMAN AND COMPANY

Excerpt from "Hamilton, Alexander" in the *Encyclopaedia Britannica,* © *Encyclopaedia Britannica,* 1967, Vol. 11, published by Encyclopaedia Britannica, Inc., reprinted by permission. Excerpts from *Bibliographic Index, Biography Index, Book Review Digest, Essay and General Literature Index, Reader's Guide to Periodical Literature,* and *Social Sciences and Humanities Index to Periodicals* [formerly *International Index to Periodicals*], reproduced by permission of The H. W. Wilson Company. Excerpt from *Subject Guide to Books in Print, 1966,* reprinted from *Subject Guide to Books in Print, 1966.* Copyright © 1966 by R. R. Bowker Company, 1180 Avenue of the Americas, New York, N.Y. 10036. Excerpt from *Dissertation Abstracts,* Vol. 24, 1963–64, pp. 185 and 1151, reprinted by permission of University Microfilms Library Services. Excerpt from *The New York Times Index,* © 1959 by The New York Times Company, reprinted by permission. Excerpt from *An Index to Book Reviews in the Humanities* (1962) reprinted by permission of Phillip Thomson, Publisher. Excerpt from "Melville's *Billy Budd* as 'An Inside Narrative,'" by William Braswell reprinted from *American Literature,* XXIX (May 1957), 138–139, by permission of Duke University Press and the author. Excerpts from Herman Melville's *Billy Budd, Sailor (An Inside Narrative),* ed. H. Hayford and M. M. Sealts, Jr., copyright © 1962 by The University of Chicago Press, reprinted by permission of The University of Chicago Press. Excerpt from "Expediency and Absolute Morality in *Billy Budd*" by Wendell Glick, reprinted by permission of the Modern Language Association from *PMLA,* LXVIII (March 1953), 104. Excerpt from "Among School Children" by W. B. Yeats, reprinted by permission of The Macmillan Company, Mr. M. B. Yeats, and Macmillan & Co. Ltd., from *Collected Poems* by W. B. Yeats. Copyright 1928 by The Macmillan Company, renewed 1956 by Georgie Yeats. Chart from "Cognitive Aspects of Psychomotor Performance" by Edwin A. Locke and Judith F. Bryan, reprinted by permission of the American Psychological Association and Edwin A. Locke. Chart from "Pattern in Language" by Anna H. Live, reprinted from *JGE: The Journal of General Education,* XVIII (July 1966), 94, by permission of that journal. Chart from "Stability of the California Short Form Test . . ." by Carmen J. Finley et al., reprinted from the *California Journal of Educational Research* by permission of that journal. Chart from "Toxigenicity of *Clostridium histolyticum*" by Shoki Nishida and M. Imaizumi, reprinted from J. Bacteriology 91:481, 1966 by permission of the American Society for Microbiology.

Library of Congress Catalog Card #67-24706

Copyright © 1967 by Scott, Foresman and Company, Glenview, Illinois 60025. All rights reserved.

Printed in the United States of America.

Regional offices of Scott, Foresman and Company are located at Atlanta, Dallas, Glenview, Palo Alto, and Oakland, N.J.

TABLE OF CONTENTS

PREFACE

In writing this manual, I have had three aims: (1) to tell the beginning researcher everything that he needs to know when he sits down to write a paper: everything from the kind of paper to use, margins, and other mechanical details, to how to choose a topic, organize his paper functionally, and write clear expository prose; (2) to direct the material to *all* undergraduate students, those in biology, for example, as well as in freshman English; and (3) to adhere to the principles of documentation and style set forth by the *MLA Style Sheet*.

In recent years an increasing number of literary journals have adopted the *MLA Style Sheet*; yet the stipulations of the University of Chicago *Manual of Style* remain a dominant force on college campuses. The same principle applies in the sciences where form and style of journals is now dictated by such works as the *Style Manual for Biological Journals* and the *Publication Manual of the American Psychological Association*. If we ask our students to read the learned journals, we should also, it seems to me, ask them to document their own papers in a fashion similar to, let us say, the *Journal of Bacteriology* for a biology paper or *PMLA* for a literature study. Moreover, the 1950–1951 Executive Council of the Modern Language Association, in a resolution reprinted on p. 2 of the *MLA Style Sheet,* said in part:

> We now earnestly hope that the *MLA Style Sheet* will be widely, even universally, used in the fields of the modern languages and literatures, that it will be carefully studied by every practicing scholar, and that graduate students will be instructed early to follow its practical recommendations. There is no longer any excuse for teaching future scholars one way to prepare term papers and theses when there is clearly another, different way in which, eventually, they must prepare manuscripts for publication.

College professors who arrive at these same conclusions and who wish to adopt the MLA style discover with dismay that a comprehensive research manual, actually based upon the *MLA Style Sheet*, is unavailable. This manual is intended to fill that vacuum.

Equally important, this manual is not a mere mechanical guide to documentation, nor is it a book of rhetoric. Rather, it gives a comprehensive treatment of *all* problems that face the beginning researcher. For instance, Chapter I tells him how to choose a restricted topic and write a thesis sentence. Next he is shown the mechanics of writing bibliography cards, since he must have this skill before entering the reference room of the library. Thereupon, Chapter III directs him, step by step, to the important reference works in the library. Supplementing this section is a separate appendix (pp. 149–170) that lists reference books and journals separated by disciplines (art, applied science, biological science, business, and so on).

Thereafter, the student is shown note-taking methods—summary, précis, paraphrase, and direct quotation. Then Chapter V explains the rhetoric of research writing (e.g., outlining, paragraph unity, word choice) and the mechanics of format (e.g., title page, margins, indentation). This chapter also includes a complete specimen research paper. Next, the chapters on footnoting and the bibliography provide over 200 sample entries, including items not often found in research manuals, such as sample entries for source books, recordings, and personal letters.

Chapter VIII, directed toward the science student, shows variations of both the "year and date" system and the "number" system. In addition, it provides 42 sample entries for biology, botany, geology, mathematics, physics, psychology, and zoology.

And to offer instruction that did not fit logically into preceding sections of the manual, I have included a glossary (pp. 139–148) that explains additional research terms not included in the text—that is, everything from accents and arabic numerals to illustrations. Finally, an exact, detailed index quickly directs the student to his desired information.

In conclusion, I wish to extend my thanks to the following persons who made this book possible: my wife Martha and sons Jim and Mark, for their love and patience; Theodore C. Owen, for his encouragement and counsel; William R. Elkins, for reading the manuscript; Verne Reaves, for his editorial assistance; Janice Kramer and Diane Meyer, for their contribution to the sample research paper; Tom Ladwig and Carl Hoffmans, for publishing the original version; and numerous members of the faculty of Kansas State Teachers College, for giving generously of their time and talents—especially those who contributed to the list of reference works: Elton Amburn, Herman Baehr, Dale M. Garvey, Robert L. Hampton, John S. Kudlacek, John Lehman, George Milton, B. A. Nugent, Alvin N. Rusk, J. T. Sandefur, Ted E. Surdy, David E. Travis, and Kathryn Whitten.

Emporia, Kansas
1967

J. D. L.

THE PRELIMINARIES

Introduction

The research paper is a type of disciplined writing that will enable you to add to your own store of knowledge and to that of others by making an intensive study of a limited topic. It involves collecting and investigating facts and opinions about the topic from numerous sources, and then using them, in an intelligently precise fashion, to provide an answer to some scholarly problem or question.

The topic of a research paper may often be one which, at least initially, you know very little about. At first the task may appear insurmountable: sources to be located, books and articles to be read, note-taking, footnoting of source material, outlining of the paper, writing, rewriting, typing, and proofreading. Perhaps at this point you will begin to question your ability to express yourself in English at all!

Obviously, some kind of orderly process must be applied to the above procedure. This book will help you do that: it outlines the basic research techniques you will need. But of course there is more to writing a good research paper than mere mechanics. Any adequate research assignment asks you to make a definite point, to inform and interest the reader. Once you have found and arranged the material for your paper, you must be able to judge critically the merit of your collected evidence and then be able to arrive at and express demonstrable conclusions about it. Such a task requires concentration and, more importantly, it demands an imaginative molding and adapting of the material. This book will also help you do that: it explains the particular writing style necessary for the presentation of your research findings.

In this respect, it is all too easy to submit a poor manuscript. For example, you might attempt to compile a paper by paraphrasing a few authorities and by inserting quotations abundantly. But such a compilation would prove seriously inadequate since it would merely be presenting commonplace facts and opinions in a research paper format. The thesis of such a paper—if indeed there was one—would not be explored or developed. In other words, you would have offered a recital of investigations without the commentary that is the ultimate purpose of all research writing.

To repeat: a research paper asks you to make a point. Here is what one noted scholar has to say about this aspect of the researcher's responsibility to his reader:

> It is our duty because we ought to be kind to our fellow creature; it is [in] our interest because if the view that we wish to put before him is clearly and competently expressed, so that he understands without trouble what we are trying to say, he will be gratified at the smooth working of his own intelligence and will inevitably think better of our theory and of its author than if he had had to puzzle himself over what we mean and then in the end doubt whether his brains are quite what they used to be![1]

In other words, writers of research papers should have the desire and the ability to make a point that will interest and inform the reader.

Research techniques and the ability to shape the material derived from research—these are two of the more important aspects of writing your paper. Along with these, you will also need to acquire a working familiarity with library resources. A college graduate is not expected to know everything; but he should possess the ability to find accurate information about any subject. Self-reliant library research and competent writing will be among your more valuable assets in meeting several kinds of demands: assignments in other courses, reports and studies for business and industry, research articles for publication, and graduate study.

Choosing a Topic

Perhaps the most important advice that can be given you is to select a topic that will be of interest to yourself and to the class. This choice requires more than passing attention; otherwise, you may discover, too late, that your impulsive choice has led you into disappointing results.

In addition, you should observe several other principles in the selection of a topic. First, the topic should be one for which ample reference material is available. Genuine research requires a variety of trustworthy sources. It should demand, therefore, much more than an investigation of one major reference book and one or two encyclopedias. Such limited materials, which will provide a report at most, are not suitable for investigative research. For example, subjects such as "Poetic Meter," "Auto Production in 1967," or "Traffic Death Tolls"

---

[1] Ronald B. McKerrow, "Form and Matter in the Publication of Research," *RES*, XVI (1940), 117.

would not be suitable as research topics because all references would provide almost identical information, and you would have little opportunity for the formulation of judgments.

Next, the topic should be one that has been examined and appraised by critics, experts, and authorities in the field. It should not, therefore, be too new. For example, a news item in this week's newspaper might appear interesting, but research materials would be limited to recent articles, editorials, and columns, providing little depth for development. You should remember, moreover, that the library consists mainly of books and magazines. Accordingly, the subject chosen must be well enough established to have received attention in these works.

A regional topic is permissible if it centers around a region where you live. For example, a student living in Mississippi might choose to write about racial tension in his state. But if you were doing the study of Mississippi while living in Illinois, you would face insurmountable obstacles in gathering materials through interlibrary loans or by expensive travel to Mississippi.

Furthermore, the research paper should usually be nontechnical. A subject that involves technical information is often beyond a beginning writer's ability because of difficult terms and concepts. That is, you should try to avoid topics such as "The Salk Vaccine," "The Xerox Discovery," or "The Apollo Spacecraft" (with this last, the topic is also too recent; the material is, perhaps, classified and unavailable).

Next, the work should be objective in tone. Bias has no place in the research paper. Your thorough examination of all the available evidence should result in responsible, impartial findings. Of course, almost all topics are controversial to some degree; so you should always guard against unsubstantiated personal opinion and prejudice. You might, for example, write about federal aid to education, but careful assimilation and presentation of the evidence would be required to prevent the appearance in your paper of prejudice and unfounded rationalization. Similarly, you would have to use extreme caution in your assessment of findings about such topics as "Protest Demonstrations," "Prayer in Public Schools," or "Urban Renewal."

Other topics to be avoided are: summary, a mere restatement of general material; straight biography, which is usually only summary (though acceptable topics may be developed on the influence of a period of life upon a person or on one aspect of a man's work); sensational topics, such as "The Murder of John F. Kennedy"; a topic that is too broad, such as "The U.S. Presidency"; or one that is not scholarly —there is seldom any place in research writing for such topics as "Fishing for Trout" or "The American Hot Dog."

Finally, you should select a topic that will permit you to form judgments and opinions which you will substantiate and support by authori tative reference material.

In brief, research study demands an evaluation, a formulation of judgments, and a demonstrable conclusion. The topic chosen must offer an opportunity for full development of each of these three points.

Preliminary Reading

You will need a thorough acquaintance with your material before attempting to restrict the subject. Your introductory reading will therefore serve several purposes: it will provide an overview of the subject; it will furnish the beginning of a working bibliography (see pp. 9–14); it will enable you to determine the availability of relevant reference material; and it will make possible a judicious restriction of the subject.

This preliminary reading does not normally require note-taking, since you cannot yet be certain of your needs. As a starting point, you might begin with a book or journal article recommended by your instructor or librarian (see pp. 15–34 for a full discussion of the use and resources of the library). You might also start with a general survey, such as *Literary History of the United States* (see Appendix II, pp. 149–170, for a list of general reference works and journals in your field). Or, you may begin with an encyclopedia, a biographical dictionary, or some other general reference work, as listed below:

ENCYCLOPEDIAS

> *Chambers's Encyclopaedia.* New ed. 15 vols. New York, 1950.
> *Collier's Encyclopedia.* 24 vols. New York, 1965.
> *Columbia Encyclopedia.* 3rd ed. New York, 1963.
> *Encyclopaedia Britannica.* 14th ed. 24 vols. Chicago, 1966.
> *Encyclopedia Americana.* 30 vols. New York, 1963.

BIOGRAPHICAL DICTIONARIES
Universal

Deceased

> *Chambers's Biographical Dictionary.* New ed. London, 1961.
> *Webster's Biographical Dictionary.* 1st ed. Springfield, Mass., 1943.

Living

Current Biography. New York, 1940–date.
A Dictionary of Universal Biography of All Ages and People. Ed. Albert M. Hyamson. 2nd ed. New York, 1951.
International Who's Who. London, 1935–date.
Twentieth Century Authors: A Biographical Dictionary of Modern Literature. Ed. Stanley J. Kunitz and Howard Haycraft. New York, 1942. Supplement, 1955.
Webster's Biographical Dictionary. 1st ed. Springfield, Mass., 1943.
World Biography. 5th ed. 2 vols. Bethpage, N.Y., 1954.

American

Deceased

Appleton's Cyclopaedia of American Biography. Ed. J. G. Wilson and John Fiske. 7 vols. New York, 1887–1900.
Dictionary of American Biography. 20 vols. New York, 1928–1937.
National Cyclopaedia of American Biography. New York, 1892–date. (In progress.)
Who Was Who in America. 3 vols. Chicago, 1951–1960.

Living

National Cyclopaedia of American Biography. New York, 1892–date. (In progress.)
Who's Who in America. Chicago, 1899–date.
Who's Who of American Women. Chicago, 1958–date.

British

Deceased

Dictionary of National Biography. Ed. Leslie Stephen and Sidney Lee. 63 vols. London, 1885–1901. Reissued in 22 vols., London, 1908–1909. Supplements to 1950.
Who Was Who [1897–1960]. London, 1920–date. (In progress.)

Living

Who's Who. London, 1849–date.

ALMANACS AND YEARBOOKS

The American Yearbook: A Record of Events and Progress. New York, 1925–date.
The Americana Annual: An Encyclopedia of Current Events. New York, 1923–date.
The Annual Register: A Review of Public Events at Home and Abroad. London, 1758–date.
Britannica Book of the Year. Chicago, 1938–date.
Collier's Year Book. New York, 1939–date.
Facts on File: A Weekly Synopsis of World Events. New York, 1940–date.
Information Please Almanac. New York, 1947–date.
Kane, Joseph N. *Famous First Facts: A Record of First Happenings, Discoveries and Inventions in the United States.* 3rd ed. New York, 1964.
The New International Year Book: A Compendium of the World's Progress, 1907–. New York, 1908–date.
The Statesman's Year-Book: Statistical and Historical Annual of the States of the World, 1864–. London, 1864–date.
The World Almanac and Book of Facts. New York, 1868–date.
Yearbook of the United Nations. Lake Success, N. Y., 1947–date.

ATLASES AND GAZETTEERS

Adams, James T. *Atlas of American History.* New York, 1943.
Atlas of World History. Ed. R. R. Palmer. Chicago, 1957.
Bartholomew, John W. *Advanced Atlas of Modern Geography.* 3rd ed. New York, 1956.
Collier's World Atlas and Gazetteer. New York, 1953.
Columbia-Lippincott Gazetteer of the World. Ed. Leon E. Seltzer. New York, 1962.
Encyclopaedia Britannica World Atlas. Chicago, 1963.
Goode's World Atlas. Ed. Edward B. Espenshade. 12th ed. Chicago, 1964.

Macmillan World Gazetteer and Geographical Dictionary. Ed. T. C. Collocott and J. O. Thorne. Rev. ed. New York, 1961.

National Geographic Atlas of the World. Ed. M. B. Grosvenor. Washington, D.C., 1963.

Shepherd, W. R. *Historical Atlas.* 8th ed. New York, 1956.

The Times Atlas of the World. Ed. John W. Bartholomew. Mid-century edition. 5 vols. London, 1955–1959.

DICTIONARIES

The American College Dictionary. Rev. ed. New York, 1965.

Fowler, Henry W., and F. G. Fowler, eds. *The Concise Oxford Dictionary of Current English.* 5th ed. rev. by E. McIntosh. Oxford, 1964.

Funk and Wagnalls New Practical Standard Dictionary of the English Language. New York, 1957.

Funk and Wagnalls Standard Dictionary of Folklore, Mythology, and Legend. 2 vols. New York, 1949–1950.

Murray, James A. H., et al., eds. *Oxford English Dictionary.* 12 vols. and supplement. Oxford, 1933.

Random House Dictionary of the English Language: The Unabridged Edition. Ed. Jess Stein. New York, 1966.

The Shorter Oxford English Dictionary. Ed. William Little et al. 3rd ed. Oxford, 1955.

Webster's New World Dictionary of the American Language. New York, 1960.

Webster's Seventh New Collegiate Dictionary. Springfield, Mass., 1963.

Webster's Third New International Dictionary of the English Language. Springfield, Mass., 1961.

Weekley, Ernest. *A Concise Etymological Dictionary of Modern English.* Rev. ed. New York, 1952.

BOOKS OF USAGE, SYNONYMS, AND DIALECT

Berrey, Lester V., and Melvin Van den Bark. *American Thesaurus of Slang.* 2nd ed. New York, 1953.

A Dictionary of American English on Historical Principles. Ed. Sir William Craigie and J. R. Hulbert. 4 vols. Chicago, 1936–1944.

A Dictionary of Americanisms on Historical Principles. Ed. Mitford M. Mathews. 2 vols. Chicago, 1951.

Fowler, H. W. *A Dictionary of Modern English Usage.* 2nd ed. rev. by Sir Ernest Gowers. Oxford, 1965.

Nicholson, Margaret. *Dictionary of American-English Usage: Based on Fowler's Modern English Usage.* New York, 1957.

Partridge, Eric. *A Dictionary of Slang and Unconventional English.* 5th ed. New York, 1961.

Perrin, Porter G. *Writer's Guide and Index to English.* 4th ed. rev. by Karl W. Dykema and Wilma R. Ebbitt. Chicago, 1965.

Roget's Thesaurus of English Words and Phrases. New ed. rev. by Robert A. Dutch. New York, 1964.

Webster's Dictionary of Synonyms. Springfield, Mass., 1942.

Wentworth, Harold. *American Dialect Dictionary.* New York, 1944.

This initial reading need not be extensive since it is intended to provide only a general survey. You will have accomplished your purpose in preliminary reading when you have enough understanding of your material to decide on the restricted phase of it which you wish to pursue.

Restricting the Subject

The effectiveness of a research paper depends mainly upon the support you are able to provide for your judgments and opinions. Detailed treatment of a topic requires you to probe deeply and to present accurate facts and ideas that demonstrate the validity of your contentions. This is one reason why you cannot afford to be too ambitious in what you attempt to cover. Another reason why your topic should be limited to a specific problem or question is that the research paper is a comparatively short work, often no more than about ten typewritten pages in length, excluding title page, outline, and bibliography. The subject should therefore be one that can be handled within these limitations of space, not one that would require twenty or thirty pages for adequate presentation.

Furthermore, you will realize no sense of accomplishment if you present only vague, indefinite statements about a too-extensive, too-generalized subject. For example, most students would not be capable of dealing adequately with "Edgar Allan Poe: His Poetic Genius," but they should get along well with "The Role of the Narrator in 'The Raven.'" Rather than attempting "The American Metropolis," you might write on "The Decline in Unskilled Jobs." And though "The Fur Trade in Frontier America" is probably unmanageable, "A Comparison of the Trapper with the Cowboy as a Frontier Type" might well be within your range.

This restriction of subject requires meticulous study of all available sources. For example, let us say you are assigned the general subject area of the U.S. Presidency. A first step in restriction could be to limit the topic to U.S. Presidents of the twentieth century. Preliminary readings might then suggest a study of one President—John F. Kennedy. You would discover, however, that there is an overwhelming amount of written data about Kennedy. Therefore, you should limit yourself to one aspect of Kennedy's administration—for example, the Cuban missile crisis. At this point you should read the related documents, articles, and books, noting particularly all material about the crisis. You might then decide that Kennedy's major decisions were of utmost importance; therefore, the topic could now read, "Kennedy's Decisions in the Cuban Missile Crisis." Such a restricted topic could probably be handled adequately in an undergraduate paper. You may also discover, of course, that further restriction is possible after note-taking is completed and you are well in command of your material. It is usually only the uninformed, uncertain writer who feels he must take refuge in the "safety" of a large, generalized, unrestricted subject.

Forming a Thesis Sentence

The next great influence upon the success of your work is your ability to limit further the scope of your study with a preliminary thesis sentence. Now that you are progressing more deeply into the subject, you should realize that your completed study will need the unity of a central purpose. Consequently, you should write, in one sentence, a statement of the controlling idea that will unite your various findings. This thesis will thus serve as the nerve center of your paper: it will be amplified and developed with every word, sentence, and paragraph of the study.

The earlier the thesis is formulated, the earlier will a satisfactory working limitation be set on note-taking. However, the thesis sentence may be changed as you progress in the study. You should not bind yourself, early in your work, to a thesis you cannot support or do not believe. In fact, the final, official thesis cannot be properly stated until after note-taking is completed. Nevertheless, a preliminary central idea will aid in the organization of facts, limit the note-taking, and eliminate needless research.

Questions often aid in the discovery of a thesis, but the thesis itself should be a declarative statement. For example, the Kennedy topic above might offer this question: "What motivated Kennedy in his actions and decisions during the Cuban missile crisis?" And such a question might lead to the following thesis statement: "Kennedy's decisions in the Cuban missile crisis reveal his strong determination to protect American interests despite a threat of nuclear war." Clearly, this thesis limits the study to an investigation of Kennedy's interest in the American position, rather than to, say, a detailed examination of Castro's actions, of Khrushchev's decisions, of the naval blockade, or of the arms build-up. In other words, you would now have a workable subject that could be handled within the limitations of space set by the instructor. More significantly, you would have given definite direction to your study.

II

THE WORKING BIBLIOGRAPHY

Early in your study, you should begin the development of a working bibliography. That is, you should begin to compile references which you will eventually investigate as possible source material.

The development of your working bibliography will continue throughout preliminary reading and note-taking. Therefore, during your preliminary reading, you should begin writing bibliography cards for references that you may wish to study later during your note-taking period. In other words, you should watch for footnotes and bibliographies that list new source material. Most books of critical evaluation will contain extensive bibliographies at the end of chapters or at the end of the book. Journal articles usually have footnotes at the bottom of the page and a bibliography at the end of the article. And the general reference works, such as encyclopedias and biographical dictionaries, will normally offer brief bibliographies at the end of each entry.

Suppose, for instance, that your topic concerns some aspect of Alexander Hamilton's political theories. Your preliminary reading of, let us say, *Encyclopaedia Britannica* will uncover not only a brief biography but also the following bibliography:

See also references under "Hamilton, Alexander," in the Index volume.

BIBLIOGRAPHY.—The most satisfactory complete biography, particularly strong on Hamilton's public career, is John C. Miller, *Alexander Hamilton: Portrait in Paradox* (1959). The most scholarly study is Broadus Mitchell, *Alexander Hamilton*, 2 vols. (1957, 1962). Nathan Schachner, *Alexander Hamilton* (1946) is a short, well-balanced and readable study. For an extended essay on Hamilton's economic and political ideas, see Louis M. Hacker, *Alexander Hamilton in the American Tradition* (1957); for careful selections of Hamilton's writings on various subjects interspersed with editorial comment, see Richard B. Morris, ed., *Alexander Hamilton and the Founding of the Nation* (1957); Broadus Mitchell, *Heritage From Hamilton* (1957); and Saul K. Padover, ed., *The Mind of Alexander Hamilton* (1958). Publication of a multi-volume work, *The Papers of Alexander Hamilton*, edited by H. C. Syrett and J. E. Cooke, began in 1961. See also David Loth, *Alexander Hamilton: Portrait of a Prodigy* (1939); Henry Jones Ford, *Alexander Hamilton* (1920); Allan M. Hamilton, *The Intimate Life of Alexander Hamilton* (1910); Frederick S. Oliver, *Alexander Hamilton: an Essay on American Union* (1906); Gertrude Atherton's interesting novel on Hamilton, *The Conqueror* (1902); William Graham Sumner, *Alexander Hamilton* (1890); Henry Cabot Lodge, *Alexander Hamilton* (1882); John T. Morse, Jr., *The Life of Alexander Hamilton*, 2 vol. (1876); and the works of Hamilton's son, John C. Hamilton, *The Life of Alexander Hamilton*, 2 vol., (1840–41), an unfinished biography that goes only to 1787, and his valuable but uncritical *History of the Republic of the United States of America, as Traced in the Writings of Alexander Hamilton*, 7 vol., 3rd ed. (1868). (A. De C.)

HAMILTON, ANTHONY (*c.* 1645–1719), French writer,

Fig. 1: From
Encyclopaedia Britannica

Since several of these sources will appear promising, you will want to begin making bibliography cards, such as:

Fig. 2: Sample
Bibliography Card

> Miller, John C. *Alexander Hamilton: Portrait in Paradox.*
>
> 1959.

Later, at the card catalog, you can insert the proper library call number (see pp. 27–31) and the place of publication. Then, when you are ready to study this particular book, your card provides the information for finding it. In addition, this card contains the necessary data for your final bibliography.

A word of caution, however. You should recognize that adding to the bibliography during preliminary reading and during note-taking is only incidental to your main bibliographical development. After preliminary reading and your selection of a restricted topic, you will need to investigate thoroughly all avenues of approach to the subject. To that end, you should follow the procedures set forth in Chapter III, "The Library" (pp. 15–34), which directs you to the important bibliographies and indexes in your library's reference room. In these books you will discover a vast array of source material. Your stack of bibliography cards will grow rapidly, providing a valuable index to the range and scope of past and recent scholarship related to your subject.

As you discover each new reference, you should record the bibliographical data onto *individual* cards. (Normally, 3 x 5 cards are used; for taking notes, 4 x 6 note cards are usual.) You should also check carefully to make certain that each bibliography card includes the following:

1. *Author's name,* followed by a period. Arrange the name in inverted order, surname first, for alphabetizing purposes. Provide the name in

the fullest form available, e.g., "Hart, Tom P.," not "Hart, T. P."

2. *Title of the work.* Underline titles of books, journals, magazines, and newspapers. Titles of periodicals may be abbreviated. Titles of books are followed by a period; titles of periodicals by a comma. Titles of articles or chapters are placed before the principal title and are placed within quotation marks; also, this entry requires a comma inside the final quotes.

3. *Publication information.* For a book: the place, followed by a comma; the date, followed by a period. For a journal: the volume number, in roman numerals; the date, in parentheses, followed by a comma; the page (s), followed by a period.

4. *Other items of documentation* may be necessary, as shown below (see Chapter VII, pp. 117–130, for exact information about positioning these items on the card):

    a) name of the editor or translator
    b) edition used, whenever it is not the first
    c) series number
    d) number of volumes with this particular title
    e) volume number if one of two or more

5. *Library call number* of a book or magazine, placed in the upper right-hand corner of the card. This item is valuable when the material is actually needed.

6. *A personal note,* at the bottom of the card, as to the type of material to be found in this source or any special aspect it presents.

Specimen Bibliography Cards

In addition to the examples provided below, you may also study the bibliographical entries in Chapter VII:

821.91
Au 2 h

Auden, Wystan H. *Homage To Clio.* New York, 1960.

Primary source

Fig. 3: Card for an Entire Book

Fig. 4: Card for an Entire Book

> 821.91
> Au2Zs2
> Spears, Monroe K. The
> Poetry of W. H. Auden. New
> York, 1963.
>
> Contains critical discussion
> of Auden.

Fig. 5: Card for a Section of a Book

> 810.8
> M 617 ap
> Miller, Perry, ed. The
> American Puritans: Their
> Prose and Poetry. Garden
> City, N.Y., 1956.
> Has comments on Thomas
> Shepard, 143–144.

Fig. 6: Card for Introduction to a Book

> 320
> L 66Ze
> Rossiter, Clinton, and James
> Lare, eds. The Essential
> Lippmann. New York,
> 1963.
>
> Check introduction for
> comments on Lippmann.

320
L662e

Lippmann, Walter. "The Public and the People," *The Essential Lippmann*. Eds. Clinton Rossiter and James Lare. New York, 1963.
Defines "the people" on 85-87.

Fig. 7: Card for a Section of a Book

973
H25
V. 15

MacDonald, William. *Jacksonian Democracy*, 1829-1837, in *The American Nation: A History*, ed. Albert B. Hart. 28 vols. New York, 1906, XV, 43-66.

Fig. 8: Card for One Volume of Several

Churchill, Henry Stern. "United Nations Headquarters - a Description and Appraisal," *Architectural Record*, CXII (July 1952), 104-122.
On function and purpose of buildings

Fig. 9: Card for a Periodical Article

Gleckner, Robert F. "William Blake and the Human Abstract," <u>PMLA</u>, LXXVI, iv, pt. 1 (1961), 373-379.

Treats "The Divine Image" and "A Divine Image."

Fig. 10: Card for a Periodical Article

Pearsall, Robert Brainard. "The Presiding Tropes of Emily Brontë," <u>CE</u>, XXVII (January 1966), 267-273.

Inspects figurative quality of her prose to emphasize her poetic qualities.

Fig. 11: Card for a Periodical Article

Brooks, Cleanth. "The <u>Waste Land</u>: Critique of the Myth," <u>Modern Poetry and the Tradition</u>. Chapel Hill, N.C., 1939. Reprinted in <u>Storm Over The Waste Land</u>, ed. Robert E. Knoll. Chicago, 1964.

Fig. 12: Card for a Casebook Reference

III

THE LIBRARY

Now that you have an overview of your subject together with a restricted topic, a thesis sentence, and the beginning of your working bibliography, you need a system of library study that will save time and labor. This chapter suggests a step-by-step method of investigation that should produce thorough coverage of your topic: it takes you first to the bibliographies and indexes, then to the card catalog, and finally to the books and articles themselves. Following this system will ensure efficiency and skill in the preparation of your paper.

Before beginning formal research, you may wish to tour the library to learn its organization. Your tour should include the information desk, the reference room, the card catalog, the periodicals room, and the stacks (if they are open to students).

The Information Desk

Here you may receive a booklet or chart that outlines the arrangement of the library or you may discuss its facilities with a librarian. In either case, you should acquaint yourself with the special services of the library: interlibrary loans, special collections, microfilm and viewing machines, the availability of typewriters and photocopying machines, audio-visual aids, and so on.

The Reference Room

An experienced researcher usually begins his investigation in the reference room. There he gathers a list of sources from bibliographies, indexes, and other works of reference. Later, at the card catalog, he supplements his list and records call numbers. Only then does he begin serious reading for note-taking.

You may employ this same procedure. Already you should have a few bibliography cards that you recorded during your preliminary reading in encyclopedias and other general works. You should now expand this small list into a full working bibliography by consulting the bibliographies and indexes in the reference room of your library. Keep in mind, however, that these works do not provide information for note-taking. But they do list other works where you will find detailed treatment of your topic. They direct you to books, pamphlets, and articles in collections, magazines, and newspapers. Also, some indexes specialize in one type of source (for example, *Readers' Guide to Periodical Literature* indexes magazines only). Other indexes specialize in one field (for example, *Education Index, Bibliography of American Literature,* and *Dramatic Bibliography*).

A word of caution, however. Bibliographies and indexes classify their listings according to individual systems that vary from work to work. Before using any index, you should study its preliminary pages to determine its system of abbreviations, symbols, and classification. And, since indexes appear weekly, bi-monthly, monthly, and yearly, you should look closely at the date of publication of each one you select. For example, if your topic concerns a contemporary problem, you would probably want to start your investigation with the most recent listings.

Because reference works must serve many students, you must not take them from the library. Rather, you should read them in the reference room, leaving them on the table so that the librarians may return them to their proper position on the shelves.

BIBLIOGRAPHIES

You will find bibliographies published separately or within such other works as encyclopedias, general reference books, critical and biographical studies, and scholarly journals. Also, you will note two types: standard bibliographies, which list sources in existence for some time, and current bibliographies, which list recent publications.

As a beginning researcher, you need a comprehensive listing of reference materials in your subject field. To that end, Appendix II of this manual contains lists of reference works and journals in the following subject areas: applied sciences (pp. 149–151), art (pp. 151–153), biological sciences (pp. 153–154), business (pp. 154–155), education (pp. 155–156), English language and literature (pp. 156–157), foreign languages (pp. 158–159), health and physical education (pp. 159–160), home economics (pp. 160–161), music (pp. 161–163), philosophy (p. 163), psychology (pp. 163–164), religion (pp. 164–165), social sciences (pp. 165–168), and speech and drama (pp. 168–170).

In addition, you will find thorough coverage of your field in any of the following sources—that is, each of these books functions as a bibliography that offers a list of other bibliographies:[1]

> Barton, Mary N., comp. *Reference Books: A Brief Guide for Students and Other Users of the Library.* 4th ed. Baltimore, 1959.
> Murphey, Robert W. *How and Where to Look It Up.* New York, 1958.
> Shores, Louis. *Basic Reference Sources: An Introduction to Materials and Methods.* Chicago, 1954.
> Walford, Arthur J., ed. *Guide to Reference Material.* London, 1959. Supplement, 1963.
> Winchell, Constance M. *Guide to Reference Books.* 7th ed. Chicago, 1951. Supplements, 1952–1962.

Let's assume you wish to proceed with the investigation of Alexander Hamilton begun in the previous chapter. You would first examine the listings under "American History" in Appendix II of this manual or in one of the books listed above. As a result, you would find such works as:

> American Historical Association. *Guide to Historical Literature.* Ed. George F. Howe and others. New York, 1961.
> Beers, Henry Putney. *Bibliographies in American History: Guide to Materials for Research.* Rev. ed. New York, 1942.
> Handlin, Oscar, and others, eds. *Harvard Guide to American History.* Cambridge, Mass., 1954.

Examining these under the appropriate heading, you would then search for special bibliographies of Hamilton, such as:

> Ford, Paul Leicester. *Bibliotheca Hamiltoniana: A List of Books Written by, or Relating to Alexander Hamilton.* New York, 1886.

This discovery would narrow the search to a "subject" bibliography —that is, one that treats one topic exclusively.

In addition to special bibliographies, you should also examine:

> *Bibliographic Index: A Cumulative Bibliography of Bibliographies.* New York, 1938–date.

Although *Bibliographic Index* originally covered only the years 1937–1942, it is kept current by supplements. It is therefore valuable for bringing your investigation of a topic up-to-date. (Note, for instance, that the publication date for the Hamilton bibliography by P. L. Ford was 1886. You can thus see that the need often arises for more

---

[1] A work of international scope is Theodore Besterman, *A World Bibliography of Bibliographies,* 4th ed. (Lausanne, 1965).

current material.) Sample entries from *Bibliographic Index* and a supplement follow:

Fig. 13: From
Bibliographic Index
1. Subject heading
2. Entry of book
that contains a
Hamiltonian bibli-
ography 3. Specific
pages on which
bibliography is
located

Fig. 14: From
Supplement to
Bibliographic Index

You will note that each entry in *Bibliographic Index* directs you to the specific bibliographic section within a critical study. In other words, by consulting this text, you would have discovered not only the four books about Hamilton but also four additional bibliographic lists. For example, a bibliography on Alexander Hamilton will be found in Broadus Mitchell's *Alexander Hamilton,* published by Macmillan in 1957 and 1962, on pages 647–666 of volume 1 and pages 775–792 of volume 2.

Another reference aid of this general nature is *Bulletin of Bibliography and Magazine Notes* (Boston, 1897–date). The first page of each volume contains an index.

TRADE BIBLIOGRAPHIES

You may also have occasion to use the trade bibliographies, which are works intended primarily for use by booksellers and librarians. You will find them helpful in three ways: to discover sources which may not be listed in other bibliographies or in the card catalog of your library; to locate facts of publication, such as place and date; and to learn if a book is in print.

Certainly, you should become familiar with *Books in Print* (New York, 1948 – date). This work provides an author-title index to the *Publishers' Trade List Annual* (New York, 1874 – date), a list of books currently in print. Also, *Publishers' Weekly* (New York, 1872 – date) offers current publication data. In addition, *Subject Guide to Books in Print* (New York, 1957 – date) supplies a subject index that enables you to discover new sources. For example, the 1966 edition contains the following entry:

```
        HAMDEN, CONN. — HISTORY
Hartley, Rachel M. History of Hamden, Connecticut, 1786-1959. il. 1943. 7.50.
  Shoe String                                                              —1
   HAMILTON, ALEXANDER  1757-1804                                          —2
Aly, Bower. Rhetoric of Alexander Hamilton. 1965. 6.50. Russell
American Philosophical Society. Commemoration of the two hundredth
  anniversary of the birth of Alexander Hamilton, 1757. (Proceedings. vol.
  102, no. 2) 1958. 1.00. Am. Philos. Soc.                                 —3
Bowers, Claude G. Jefferson and Hamilton. il  1929. 7.50; sold with Young
  Jefferson, and Jefferson in power, 3 vols. 21.00. Houghton               —4
 Boyd, Julian P. Number 7. 1964. 4.00. Princeton
Caldwell, Lynton K  Administrative theories of Hamilton and Jefferson. 1964. —5
  6.50. Russell
Hacker, L. Alexander Hamilton  1957  pap. 2.75. McGraw                     —6
Hamilton, Alexander. Hamilton reader. (Docket bk) ed. by Margaret E. Hall.
  1957. 3.50. Oceana
Hamilton, Alexander. Law practice of Alexander Hamilton. vol. 1. ed. by J.
  Goebel and others. 18.50. Columbia*
Konefsky, S. J. John Marshall and Alexander Hamilton. 1964. 5.95. Macmillan
Miller, John C. Alexander Hamilton. il. 1959. 10.00. Harper
Miller, John C. Alexander Hamilton and the growth of the new nation.        —7
  (Torchbks. Tb3057  pap. 3.45. Harper*
Mitchell, Broadus. Alexander Hamilton. 2 vols. vol. 1, 10.00; vol. 2, 12.50;
  set, 20.00. Macmillan                                                    —8
Mitchell, B. Heritage from Hamilton. 1957  5.00. Columbia
Morris, Richard B., ed. Alexander Hamilton and the founding of the nation.
  1957. 7.50  Dial                                                         —9
Rossiter, Clinton. Alexander Hamilton and the Constitution. 1964. 6.75. Harcourt
Schachner, Nathan. Alexander Hamilton. 1961. pap. 2.25. Barnes, A. S.
Swanson, Donald. Origins of Hamilton's fiscal policies. 1963. pap. 2.00. U. of Fla.
Syrett, Harold C., and others, eds. Interview in Weehawken. il. 1960. 4.50.
  Wesleyan U. P.
Tipple, John. Hamilton-Jefferson. pap. 2.25. Allen, Howard

        HAMILTON, ALEXANDER, 1757-1804 — FICTION
Atherton, Gertrude. Conqueror. 1943. 5.95. Lippincott

        HAMILTON, ALEXANDER, 1757-1804 — JUVENILE LITERATURE
Crouse, Anna, and Russel. Alexander Hamilton and Aaron Burr (gr. 4-6).
```

Fig. 15: From *Subject Guide to Books in Print* 1. Subject 2. Dates of subject's life span 3. Book contains illustrations 4. Author 5. Title 6. Date of publication 7. Paperback book 8. Price 9. Publisher

In short, you cannot overlook the trade bibliographies. Others are:

Paperbound Books in Print. New York, 1955 – date.
Since the publication of paperback books is increasing annually and

since important books are occasionally found only in paperback
form, you may find this text a necessary tool.

Cumulative Book Index. Minneapolis [later New York], 1900–date.
This work lists books by author, subject, editor, and translator. Use it
to find complete publication data or to locate *all* material in English
on a particular subject.

The National Union Catalog: A Cumulative Author List. Ann Arbor, Mich.,
1953–date.
Basically, this work is the card catalog in book form; that is, it provides a list representing the Library of Congress printed cards and
also titles reported by other libraries. It supplements the *Library of
Congress Catalog.*

Library of Congress Catalog: Books: Subjects, 1950–1954. Ann Arbor,
Mich., 1955; Washington, D.C., 1956–date.
This catalog complements *The National Union Catalog* by supplying a
subject classification.

General Catalogue of Printed Books. London, 1881–date.
This British publication serves a corresponding function to *The
National Union Catalog.* Such listings are available for most nations.

Union List of Serials in Libraries of the United States and Canada. 3rd ed.
New York, 1965. Supplements, *New Series Titles,* Washington, D.C.,
1953–date.
You may consult this work to determine if a nearby library has a
magazine that is unavailable in your library.

Ulrich's Periodical Directory. Ed. Eileen C. Graves. 9th ed. New York,
1959.
This work is a guide to current periodicals, both domestic and foreign.

INDEXES

A general index furnishes the page number(s) of another book or
magazine where you will find specific information. Fundamentally,
there are three types: indexes to materials in books and collections,
indexes to literature in periodicals, and indexes to materials in newspapers.[2]

Indexes to Books and Collections

First, you should recall *Bibliographic Index* (see pp. 17–18), which
also refers you to books or collections. In addition, you should be
familiar with:

Essay and General Literature Index, 1900–1933. Comp. by Minnie E.
Sears and Marian Shaw. New York, 1934. Supplements, 1934–date.
*Biography Index: A Cumulative Index to Biographical Material in Books
and Magazines.* New York, 1946/47–date.

The first index directs you to material of a biographical and/or critical nature. Note the following entry from the 1960–1964 supplement:

[2]For a comprehensive listing of indexes, you may consult Norma O. Ireland, *An Index to Indexes*
(Boston, 1942).

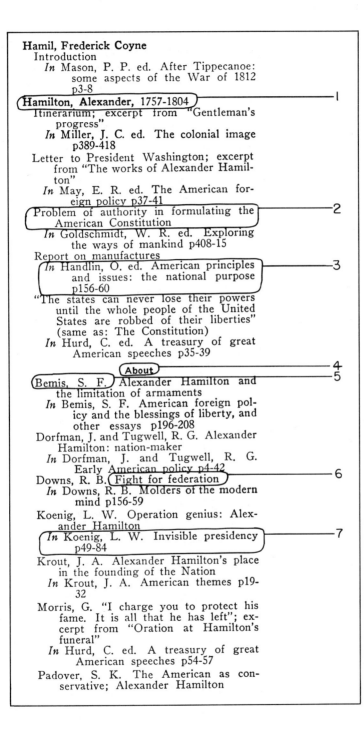

Hamil, Frederick Coyne
Introduction
  In Mason, P. P. ed. After Tippecanoe: some aspects of the War of 1812 p3-8

Hamilton, Alexander, 1757-1804 — 1
Itinerarium; excerpt from "Gentleman's progress"
  In Miller, J. C. ed. The colonial image p389-418
Letter to President Washington; excerpt from "The works of Alexander Hamilton"
  In May, E. R. ed. The American foreign policy p37-41
Problem of authority in formulating the American Constitution — 2
  In Goldschmidt, W. R. ed. Exploring the ways of mankind p408-15
Report on manufactures
  In Handlin, O. ed. American principles and issues: the national purpose p156-60 — 3
"The states can never lose their powers until the whole people of the United States are robbed of their liberties" (same as: The Constitution)
  In Hurd, C. ed. A treasury of great American speeches p35-39

About — 4
— 5
Bemis, S. F. Alexander Hamilton and the limitation of armaments
  In Bemis, S. F. American foreign policy and the blessings of liberty, and other essays p196-208
Dorfman, J. and Tugwell, R. G. Alexander Hamilton: nation-maker
  In Dorfman, J. and Tugwell, R. G. Early American policy p4-42
Downs, R. B. Fight for federation — 6
  In Downs, R. B. Molders of the modern mind p156-59
Koenig, L. W. Operation genius: Alexander Hamilton
  In Koenig, L. W. Invisible presidency p49-84 — 7
Krout, J. A. Alexander Hamilton's place in the founding of the Nation
  In Krout, J. A. American themes p19-32
Morris, G. "I charge you to protect his fame. It is all that he has left"; excerpt from "Oration at Hamilton's funeral"
  In Hurd, C. ed. A treasury of great American speeches p54-57
Padover, S. K. The American as conservative; Alexander Hamilton

Fig. 16: From *Essay and General Literature Index* 1. Subject 2. Article by Hamilton 3. Book in which Hamilton's essay appears 4. Designates that following essays are *about* Hamilton, rather than essays written *by* him 5. Author of essay about Hamilton 6. Title of the essay 7. Book in which the essay appears

As shown above, the *Essay and General Literature Index* lists writings *by* the author as well as essays *about* him. In addition, you should note, for example, that L. W. Koenig's "Operation Genius: Alexander Hamilton" will be found in L. W. Koenig's *Invisible Presidency*, published by Rinehart in 1960, on pages 49–84 (the publisher and date are found in a "List of Books Indexed" at the end of each volume of *Essay and General Literature Index*).

On the other hand, *Biography Index* is a good starting point if your study involves a famous person. It gives clues to biographical information for people of all lands. (However, for the years 1900–1947 you should see *Essay and General Literature Index*.) Note the following excerpt from *Biography Index:*

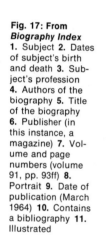

Fig. 17: From Biography Index
1. Subject 2. Dates of subject's birth and death 3. Subject's profession 4. Authors of the biography 5. Title of the biography 6. Publisher (in this instance, a magazine) 7. Volume and page numbers (volume 91, pp. 93ff) 8. Portrait 9. Date of publication (March 1964) 10. Contains a bibliography 11. Illustrated

Most indexes published by the H. W. Wilson Company use this same code system. Specifically, note the code for journal volumes and page numbers—"37:43–63." To conform to the suggestions in this manual, you will want to record this data differently on your bibliography card, as follows:

Parsons, S. H. "Continuing Crusade: Four Generations of the Adams Family View Alexander Hamilton," *NEQ*, xxxvii (4 March 1964), 43-63.

Fig. 18: Sample Bibliography Card

When looking for biographical information, you should also consult a good biographical dictionary (see pp. 4–5).

Another important index is the subject index to *Dissertation Abstracts: A Guide to Dissertations and Monographs Available in Microfilm* (Ann Arbor, Mich., 1952–date). (From 1938–1951, this work was entitled *Microfilm Abstracts*.) Issue number 12 of each volume has two parts: Part I contains the abstracts and Part II the cumulated subject and author indexes for issues 1 through 12. For example, the subject index of Volume 24, No. 12, Part II, offers the following:

HAMBURG—POLITICS AND GOVERNMENT

The politics of labor in Hamburg, 1918-192.. ·
R. A. Comfort.   **XXIV**, 3310

HAMILTON, ALEXANDER, 1757-1804

Alexander Hamilton and the British orientation
of American foreign policy, 1783-1803. H. V.
Johnson.   **XXIV**, 1151

HAMMETT EQUATION

The application of the Hammett equation to the
benzyl system. D. M. Carlton. **XXIV**, 3975

Fig. 19: From the Index to *Dissertation Abstracts*

This entry directs you to page 1151 of Volume 24 of *Dissertation Abstracts* where you will find an abstract of a dissertation by Helene Vivan Johnson. A portion of that abstract follows:

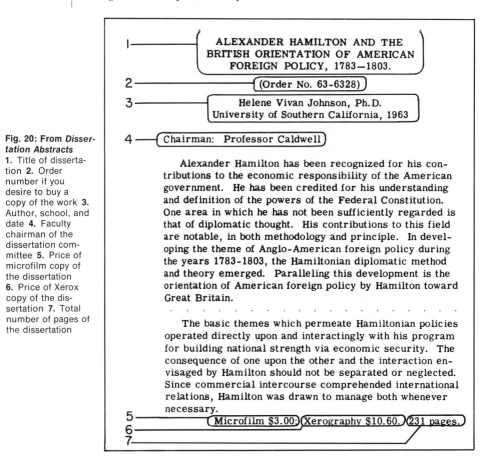

Fig. 20: From *Dissertation Abstracts*
1. Title of dissertation **2.** Order number if you desire to buy a copy of the work **3.** Author, school, and date **4.** Faculty chairman of the dissertation committee **5.** Price of microfilm copy of the dissertation **6.** Price of Xerox copy of the dissertation **7.** Total number of pages of the dissertation

1 —— ALEXANDER HAMILTON AND THE BRITISH ORIENTATION OF AMERICAN FOREIGN POLICY, 1783—1803.

2 —— (Order No. 63-6328)

3 —— Helene Vivan Johnson, Ph.D. University of Southern California, 1963

4 —— Chairman: Professor Caldwell

Alexander Hamilton has been recognized for his contributions to the economic responsibility of the American government. He has been credited for his understanding and definition of the powers of the Federal Constitution. One area in which he has not been sufficiently regarded is that of diplomatic thought. His contributions to this field are notable, in both methodology and principle. In developing the theme of Anglo-American foreign policy during the years 1783-1803, the Hamiltonian diplomatic method and theory emerged. Paralleling this development is the orientation of American foreign policy by Hamilton toward Great Britain.

The basic themes which permeate Hamiltonian policies operated directly upon and interactingly with his program for building national strength via economic security. The consequence of one upon the other and the interaction envisaged by Hamilton should not be separated or neglected. Since commercial intercourse comprehended international relations, Hamilton was drawn to manage both whenever necessary.

5 —— Microfilm $3.00. Xerography $10.60. 231 pages.
6 ——
7 ——

The abstract, of course, is only a brief summary of the entire work. If the dissertation is pertinent to your topic or if you plan an exhaustive investigation, you may wish to order a copy of the complete work from University Microfilms, Inc., Ann Arbor, Michigan. To that end, information at the end of the abstract stipulates the cost of microfilm and Xerox copies of the complete dissertation.

Indexes to Literature in Periodicals

Because they provide four types of information better than any other source, you must use articles in periodicals. Understandably, they contain: the most recent materials on any subject; obscure, temporary, or extremely new materials; the climate of opinion of a particular period; and supplements to professional literature. For example, materials often appear as journal articles before their publication in book form.

There are two main types of periodicals: general periodicals (for example, *Time, Look,* or *Ladies Home Journal*); and professional journals (for example, *National Tax Journal, Mathematical Review,* or *Journal of Psychology*). You will use both types, of course, but you should depend mainly upon the learned journals whose treatment of topics is more critically detailed.

As an index to articles in periodicals, you should first investigate:

Readers' Guide to Periodical Literature. New York, 1900–date.

A sample entry follows:

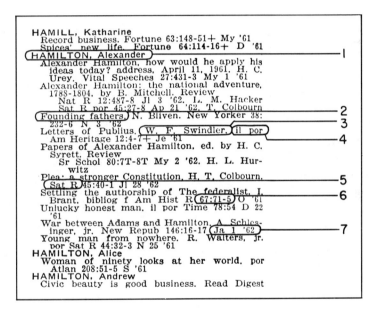

Fig. 21: From *Readers' Guide to Periodical Literature* **1.** Subject **2.** Title of article **3.** Author **4.** Illustrated with a portrait **5.** Name of magazine **6.** Volume and page numbers (volume 67, pp. 71–75) **7.** Date (January 1, 1962)

In most instances, this index directs you to general periodicals, though from 1953 on scientific periodicals have been included. If you wish to examine the scholarly journals, such as *American History Review* and *Political Science Quarterly,* you should investigate:

Social Sciences and Humanities Index [1907–date; formerly titled *International Index to Periodicals*]. New York, 1916–date.

A sample entry from *Social Sciences and Humanities Index* follows:

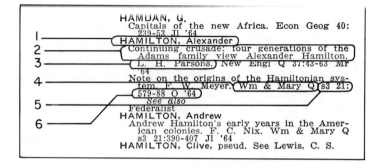

Fig. 22: From *Social Sciences and Humanities Index* **1.** Subject **2.** Title of article **3.** Authbr **4.** Name of journal **5.** Series and volume number **6.** Page numbers and date

Next, you should investigate:

Nineteenth Century Readers' Guide to Periodical Literature, 1890–1899 [with supplementary indexing, 1900–1922]. 2 vols. New York, 1944.
Poole's Index to Periodical Literature, 1802–1881. Rev. ed. Boston, 1891. Supplements cover the years 1882–1906.

> With this work you may locate information on materials from 1802–1906. Note that *Poole's Index* has only a subject classification. See, however, Marion V. Bell and Jean C. Bacon, *Poole's Index Date and Volume Key* (Chicago, 1957) for an alphabetical title listing.

Newspaper Indexes

Newspapers are an excellent source of information. Therefore, you should familiarize yourself with the *New York Times Index* (New York, 1913–date). It indexes not only the *New York Times* but also indirectly indexes most other newspapers by revealing the date on which the same news was probably reported in other newspapers. Many libraries have the *New York Times* on microfilm. A sample entry from the *New York Times Index* follows:

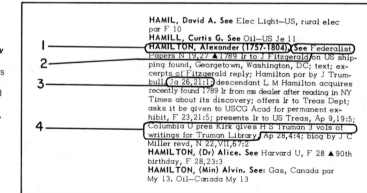

Fig. 23: From *New York Times Index* **1.** Subject **2.** Cross reference **3.** Date, page number, and column number (January 26, p. 21, column 1) **4.** Title of newspaper article

For example, the last entry on Hamilton in the *New York Times Index* is a review of J. C. Miller's biography of Hamilton which appears in the *New York Times,* November 22, Part VII, page 67, column 2 (sections of the Sunday edition are shown by a roman numeral).

For British newspapers a similar index is *Official Index* [to *The London Times*] (London, 1907–date). It is available in most American libraries.

Pamphlet Indexes

The principal index to most pamphlet material is:

Vertical File Index: A Subject and Title Index to Selected Pamphlet Material. New York, 1932/35–date.

Your library may not own many of the items listed, but the catalog gives a description of each entry, the price, and the means by which you may purchase it.

Finding the Call Number

After completing your work in the reference room, you should turn next to the card catalog, which specifies the location of all books in the library. (Most libraries have a separate, smaller catalog for periodicals.) With your bibliography cards arranged alphabetically, you can easily find and record the call number for each book. If, after exerting sufficient effort, you cannot locate a catalog card, you may seek help from a librarian.

For each book you will usually find in the catalog three separate entries (or more), filed under: (1) the author's name, printed on the first line (see p. 28); (2) the title of the work, typed in black ink at the top of the card (see p. 28); and (3) the subject, typed in red ink at the top of the card (see p. 31). Additional catalog cards are filed for coauthors, translators, editors, and illustrators, and for other subject headings.

MAIN ENTRY CARD

As you go through the card catalog you will quickly discover that there is a main entry card for each book you are seeking, usually filed under the author's name. For example:

Fig. 24: Main Entry Card (Author Card) 1. Classification number **2.** Author number **3.** Author **4.** Birth date of author **5.** Title **6.** Edition **7.** Place of publication **8.** Date of publication **9.** Publisher **10.** Technical description: size, number of pages, illustrations, etc. **11.** Note on contents of book

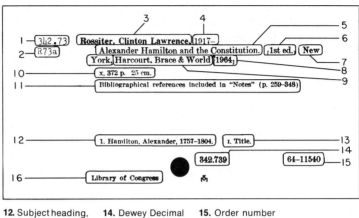

12. Subject heading, card filed under subject's name **13.** Subject heading, card filed under title of the work

14. Dewey Decimal System number

15. Order number — Library of Congress **16.** Publisher of this card

You may gather several kinds of information from this main entry card. Specifically, you should record the *complete* call number — in this case, $\frac{342.73}{R73a}$. Do not copy the first line only! You must have the full number, usually consisting of two (and sometimes three) lines of symbols. In addition, you should record any bibliographical notations, such as "Bibliographical references included in 'Notes' (p. 259 – 348)." Data of this sort can direct you to additional sources.

TITLE CARD

Another card is always filed alphabetically by the book title:

Fig. 25: Title Card 1. Title, usually typed in black ink **2.** Main entry card filed under "Hamilton, Alexander" **3.** Editor (see below, item 5) **4.** Subject headings (see Subject card, p. 31) **5.** Separate card filed under name of editor **6.** As we see, a card is filed by the title of the work **7.** Library of Congress number

330.973
H18p

Papers on public credit, commerce and finance — 1

Hamilton, Alexander, 1757-1804. — 2

Papers on public credit, commerce and finance, by Alexander Hamilton, edited by Samuel McKee, jr.) ... with a foreword by Elihu Root. New York, Columbia university press, 1934. — 3

xxiv, 3 p. l., [3]-303 p., 1 l. front. (port.) 23½ cm.

1. Finance, Public—U. S.—1789-1800. 2. Debts, Public—U. S. 3. Credit—U. S. 4. U. S.—Manuf. 5. U. S.—Comm. 6. U. S.—Pol. & govt.—1783-1800. (i. McKee, Samuel, jr., ed.) (ii. Title.) — 4, 5

HC105.H18 — 6   330.973   34—18967 — 7

Library of Congress   [57d⁸1]

A third type of card found in the catalog is the subject card—but we will come to that in a moment.

THE CALL NUMBER

The library classifies and arranges its books by the call number, which is usually a combination of the Dewey Decimal System and the Cutter Author Number. In a call number such as $\frac{330.973}{H18p}$, the first line is the Dewey Decimal Number, and the second line is the Cutter Author Number. The Dewey system divides all books into ten general classifications:

000–099	General Works
100–199	Philosophy
200–299	Religion
300–399	Social Sciences
400–499	Language
500–599	Pure Science
600–699	Technology (Applied Sciences)
700–799	The Arts
800–899	Literature
900–999	History

The Dewey system then divides each of these ten general classes into ten smaller divisions. For example, the general literature classification (800–899) is broken down into:

800–809	General Works [on Literature]
810–819	American Literature
820–829	English Literature
830–839	German Literature
840–849	French Literature
850–859	Italian Literature
860–869	Spanish Literature
870–879	Latin Literature
880–889	Greek and Classical Literature
890–899	Literature of Other Languages

Next, American Literature (810–819) is divided into the following classifications:

811	Poetry
812	Drama

813   FICTION
814   Essays
815   Speeches
816   Letters
817   Satire and Humor
818   Miscellany
819   Minor Related Literature

Further subdivisions of each of these groups separate the works of literature until a specific number is designated for each book (for example, 814.21 or 816.143).

Immediately below the Dewey classification number, most libraries also insert an author number, a set of letters and numerals based on the Cutter Three-Figure Author Table. For example, "H18p" is the author number for Alexander Hamilton, *Papers on Public Credit, Commerce and Finance.* The letter "H" is the initial of the author's last name; next, the Cutter table stipulates the arabic numeral "18"; and finally, the lower case "p" designates the first important letter in the title to distinguish this entry from other writings by Hamilton. Thus, the complete call number for Hamilton's book is $\frac{330.973}{H18p}$. You must employ both items to locate the book.

Some libraries employ the Library of Congress classification system, which features capital letters followed by arabic numerals to designate the subdivisions (for example, JK154 for *The Federalist* or E302.6 for Broadus Mitchell's *Alexander Hamilton*). The major divisions of the Library of Congress system follow:

A   General Works and Polygraphy
B   Philosophy and Religion
C   History and Auxiliary Sciences
D   History and Topography
     (excluding America)
E-F   America
G   Geography and Anthropology
H   Social Sciences
J   Political Science
K   Law
L   Education
M   Music
N   Fine Arts
P   Language and Literature
Q   Science

R Medicine
S Agriculture and Plant and Animal Husbandry
T Technology
U Military Science
V Naval Science
Z Bibliography and Library Science

Using the Catalog as an Index

The card catalog indexes all important subject areas by means of subject cards and tabular headings. This is the third kind of card to be found in the catalog. For example, if your subject is Public Debts, you would discover under "Debts, public" an index to all books in the library on this subject. Note the following subject card:

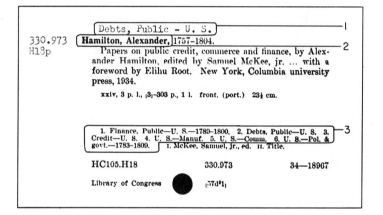

Fig. 26: Subject Card (See also "Main Entry Card," p. 28, and "Title Card," p. 28) **1.** Subject heading, usually typed in red ink **2.** Main entry card filed under "Hamilton, Alexander" **3.** Other subject headings under which you will find this same card (see below)

The library makes a subject card of this nature for every topic developed within each book. As shown above, the library will index this same book by Hamilton under these other subject headings:

> Finance, Public—U.S.—1789–1800
> Credit—U.S.
> U.S.—Manuf.
> U.S.—Comm.
> U.S.—Pol. & govt.—1783–1809

In other words, the card catalog of your library is, among other things, a subject index to the books it lists.

Other Catalog Cards

Temporary cards are of a different color and usually indicate that a book is not in circulation. However, ask the librarian about the book, for it may be available:

Fig. 27: Temporary Card

```
                                                    4–5–66

          66–384   Hamilton, Alexander
                   The works of Alexander Hamilton
                   . . . 1904.


                   Gen
                   12 v.


                      BOOK ON ORDER
                           ◯
```

Cross-reference cards refer you to alternate or related headings. There are two types. The "see" card indicates the correct heading under which material is listed:

Fig. 28: Cross-Reference Card

```
              U. S.–History–Reconstruction
                 see
              Reconstruction




                           ◯
```

The "see also" card directs you to related subjects that contain additional material:

```
Reconstruction
  see also
Southern States—History—1865—
```

Fig. 29: "See Also" Card

In short, your best procedure with the card catalog is a combination of practices: you can easily record call numbers while you search for new sources. For example, with your bibliography cards in hand, you should look first under the proper subject heading—"Hamilton," in this instance. There you will find index cards for all books *by* Hamilton and most books *about* him. At the same time, you will discover the call numbers for the majority of your sources. In addition, you may uncover new sources that supplement your working bibliography.

Getting Your Books and Periodical Articles

THE STACKS

Armed with the correct call numbers, you are now ready to locate your books in the stacks or, in the case of closed stacks, to request the books from a clerk. If a book is unavailable, you may request a "hold" on the book. When it returns, the librarian will reserve it for you.

THE RESERVE DESK

Recognizing the importance of certain books to their disciplines, many instructors place them "on reserve" in the library so that a limited number of books will be available to many students. You will want to determine if any books necessary for your research are on reserve. To that end, you should ask the clerk at the desk to explain the filing system employed.

If you use a reserve book, you must usually read it in the library. Some libraries, however, permit overnight withdrawal of reserve books. But under no circumstances should you keep such a book for several days or hide it somewhere in the library for future use. These books must serve many students.

THE PERIODICALS ROOM

You will locate periodical articles in both bound and unbound volumes. The bound ones, usually on open stacks, contain several issues within a hard cover. The unbound volumes are usually of recent publication. If periodicals are kept in closed stacks, you must provide the clerk with sufficient publication data.

Supplementing Library Materials

Without doubt the library is your best source of information when writing a research paper. But you may also find material in other places. For instance, you could write your U.S. Senator or Congressman for one of the many booklets printed by the Government Printing Office. You will find a list of these materials, many of which are free, in a monthly catalog issued by the Superintendent of Documents, *United States Government Publications Monthly Catalog*, Washington, D.C., 1895 – date.

Also important are audio-visual materials: films, filmstrips, music, phonograph recordings, slides, and tape recordings. You may find these in the library or in some other location on or off campus.

Other good sources of information are: radio and television programs, lectures, letters, public addresses, personal interviews, and questionnaires.

IV

NOTE-TAKING

After the completion of your preliminary investigation, you may direct your note-taking toward the solution or clarification of one specific problem. By this time you should have completed preliminary readings, having gained in this an initial familiarity with the range of your sources. Also, you should have framed a thesis sentence for your restricted topic, determining thereby the specific direction you will pursue in your study. In addition, you should have in hand the beginning of your working bibliography, to which you will add new references as you come upon them during the process of note-taking.

The Preliminary Outline

A well-written outline will help you ensure paragraph coherence and stylistic unity. To achieve the desired outline, you should follow several progressive steps: (1) jot down your ideas in a rough list; (2) organize a preliminary outline by categorizing your list of ideas; and (3) expand the development of your preliminary outline into a formal topic or sentence outline (see pp. 50–53 for a discussion of outline forms). In order for your selection and paraphrasing of material to contribute exactly to the scheme of your paper, you should complete items (1) and (2) before you begin taking notes. In other words, now is the time to prepare a preliminary outline. This preliminary outline should be based upon ideas that you absorbed while choosing and restricting your subject and while forming your thesis sentence or purpose statement.

Suppose, for example, that you read Herman Melville's novella *Billy Budd* and that you wrote the following purpose statement for your paper:

    The purpose of this paper is to examine Melville's use
    of biblical references in Billy Budd.

Your intentions are clear: you will examine the biblical references, searching, meanwhile, for Melville's purpose in using them. As a first step, you should list your supporting ideas in random order, as in the following:

```
Billy Budd=Adam
Billy's innocence
Claggart is evil=Satan?
Billy's fall from grace
David and Saul
Joseph and his brothers
Good and Evil
Abraham and Isaac
Vere as Abraham?
Billy as Isaac?
Are the characters symbolic?
The Bible treats good and evil
What would Vere symbolize?
```

Obviously, this list is not an outline, but you now have your ideas on paper where you may examine them and find relationships. You should now organize the items, grouping your main topics and relating subordinate elements to them. Thus, you will divide your ideas into separate categories that will, in turn, suggest the structure of your research paper. And, since you may separate your material in various ways, you should consider a few methods of organization and classification.

First, select an overall plan of procedure, either general to particular (deductive) or particular to general (inductive). If you arrange your materials deductively, you will present first a general statement that you will afterwards support with specific details and instances. For example, you might wish to state a generalization first: "President Johnson's initial escalation of the Vietnam war was necessary." You could then show that specific, successive events proved him correct. Similarly, you could use the general to particular scheme in other research papers: to state the theme of an author and to prove it with details from his writings; to present the conclusions of a laboratory experiment and to state the particulars; or to declare the dishonesty of a dictator and then to present your proof. In other papers, however, you may wish to use the particular to general order. Using this technique, you would reverse the above process and, writing inductively, present first the specifics of your argument and then work carefully toward a general conclusion.

After selecting one of the two external orders, you should consider your internal arrangement, that is, the way in which you will classify and present the various factors of your argument. Having selected, for example, a general to particular arrangement for the Vietnam topic mentioned above, you would open with a generalization, perhaps to the effect that President Johnson's initial escalation of the war was necessary for the control of Communist aggression in the Far East. You could then order your supporting material by using one or more of the methods listed below.

CAUSE AND EFFECT

You may employ cause and effect, listing, for example, reasons for President Johnson's various assumptions and decisions and/or the effects of them. In this way, you would examine the reasons why something is true or you would study the result of some action or idea. The cause and effect method of classification is effective for examining social issues, such as civil rights, school prayers, or extremist groups, and for exploring such topics as a musician's style, a biological experiment, or a pattern of psychological behavior.

COMPARISON AND CONTRAST

After examining your Vietnam topic, you might choose one of the following plans: (1) a comparison and/or contrast of President Johnson's assumptions with those of Senator J. W. Fulbright; (2) a comparison and/or contrast of the Vietnam war with the Korean War; or (3) a comparison and/or contrast of the Pentagon "hawks" with the Senate "doves." In short, you could discuss your subject in relation to another subject. In other research papers, you might compare and/or contrast two works by an artist or a poet, compare and/or contrast the political climate of one state with that of another state, or compare and/or contrast the results of two similar experiments.

SPATIAL ORDER

Spatial order is the backbone of descriptive writing. Your focus of attention moves logically from one detail to another as you describe, for example, political regions, geographic or topographic features of the land, or the design of a city, housing development, flower, chair, and so on. The Vietnam topic would require a spatial order if you examined the strategic location of Vietnam in relation to its neighbors.

CHRONOLOGICAL ORDER

With the Vietnam topic you may wish to show, chronologically, that specific, successive events have proved Johnson correct. Therefore, you would present your particulars in the order of their happening. With other research papers you could trace chronologically a literary theme through several works of an author, arrange your historical study by time sequence, or show the step-by-step method of a laboratory process. However, because you must reach judgments and conclusions about the events, you will seldom use pure narration or storytelling in writing the average research paper. In other words, even though you discuss a series of happenings, you will probably use other methods, such as cause and effect or comparison and contrast.

COMBINING THE METHODS OF ARRANGEMENT

Several of the methods of ordering your outline just discussed may be used at the same time. For example, you could arrange your Vietnam paper chronologically with three events: the sending of advisers to Vietnam, the Gulf of Tonkin incident, and the troop build-up. However, since you must also reach certain judgments within each of the three time divisions, you would probably also employ cause and effect as a subdivision, listing the causes of certain events and the resulting effects. Similarly, the "Billy Budd" preliminary outline (see below — the complete "Billy Budd" paper is on pp. 80–96) shows the writer utilizing the particular to general order by listing instances that point toward Melville's general purpose. Within each section of that outline, the writer should obviously resort to the comparison and contrast method. And he must, if he is to be successful, discuss the effect of each comparison upon Melville's general purpose. Obviously, he cannot escape an overlapping of methods. Neither can you, but if you select carefully an external plan and an internal one, the subdivisions should logically follow. (See pp. 50–54 for an additional discussion of rhetorical methods.)

ARRANGING YOUR LIST OF IDEAS

Looking again at the list of ideas above (p. 36) for the "Billy Budd" paper, you can see that the biblical allusions will form the core of the sample preliminary outline. This preliminary outline might appear as follows:

```
I.    Good and evil--the Bible and Billy Budd
II.   Billy and Adam
III.  David and Saul--Billy and Claggart
IV.   Joseph and his brothers
V.    Abraham and Isaac
VI.   Characters symbolize good = Billy
                           evil = Claggart
                              ? = Vere
```

Brief as it is, such an outline as this one will help you locate and record the important, necessary data and omit information that looks valuable but that, in fact, contributes little to your overall plan. The outline is ragged and incomplete, but only you will see it. Such a preliminary outline represents roughly the best you can do before note-taking.

Moreover, you should not feel bound to this first outline. Instead, let it develop and grow; add new topics and discard others, rearrange your order, evaluate topics, and subordinate minor elements. In short, as your ideas materialize, you should allow your outline to expand accordingly. (Before writing your final outline, however, see pp. 50–53.)

Examining Your Source Material

You need not, of course, read everything, but you should skim all potentially relevant material to determine its relationship to your thesis and rough outline. Upon discovery of pertinent information, you can then write accurate, detailed notes. But again, you should record only that material which will aid the development and clarification of your thesis.

Also, you should closely examine each book to see if it contains, in addition to its text, any of the following: a table of contents, preface, introduction, index, glossary, appendix, footnotes, or bibliography. By reading a table of contents, for example, you might discover that only one chapter of a book treats your topic. An author's preface may explain the presence or absence of certain material. An introduction will include a critical overview of the book. The index of a book will help you discover whether the book discusses your subject at all. Equally important, a glossary lists and defines terms, an appendix offers additional material, and the bibliography and footnotes suggest new sources.

Finally, you should utilize the most recent, reliable sources of information. Since you are expected, always, to form sound judgments based on the merit of your collected evidence, you should closely evaluate outdated or biased material. In this regard, note that most critics discuss the judgments and opinions of other authorities. Thus, if your source refers to a certain writer as a recognized authority, a good check would be to record this fact and then carefully inspect that writer's work. When in doubt about the validity of a source, you may counsel with your instructor or consult the *Book Review Digest* (New York, 1905–date). A sample entry from a recent volume of *Book Review Digest* follows:

Fig. 3B. From Book
Review Digest **1.**
Author, title, and
facts of publication
2. Call number and
subject entry for
card catalog **3.**
Reviewer's descrip-
tion of the book **4.**
Reviewed favorably
by the reviewer **5.**
Reviewed both
favorably and
unfavorably by the
reviewer **6.** Review-
er's judgment of the
book **7.** Facts of
publication of the
review—*New York
Times Book Review*
(April 15, 1962),
p. 16 **8.** Number of
words in the
complete review

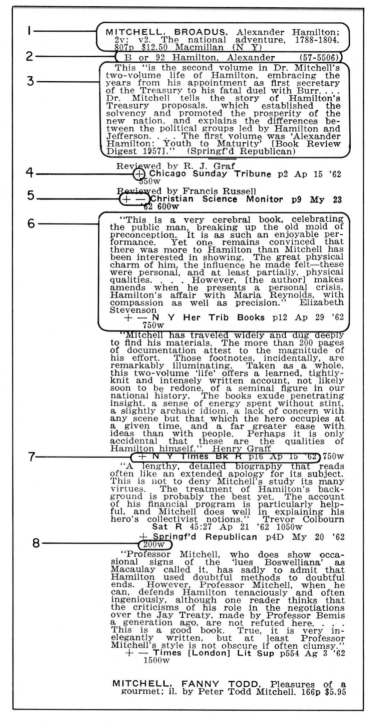

1 — **MITCHELL, BROADUS.** Alexander Hamilton; 2v; v2. The national adventure, 1788-1804. 807p $12.50 Macmillan (N Y)

2 — B or 92 Hamilton, Alexander (57-5506)

3 — This "is the second volume in Dr. Mitchell's two-volume life of Hamilton, embracing the years from his appointment as first secretary of the Treasury to his fatal duel with Burr. . . . Dr. Mitchell tells the story of Hamilton's Treasury proposals, which established the solvency and promoted the prosperity of the new nation, and explains the differences be- tween the political groups led by Hamilton and Jefferson. . . . The first volume was 'Alexander Hamilton: Youth to Maturity' [Book Review Digest 1957]." (Springf'd Republican)

Reviewed by R. J. Graf
4 — + Chicago Sunday Tribune p2 Ap 15 '62 550w

Reviewed by Francis Russell
5 — + — Christian Science Monitor p9 My 23 '62 600w

6 — "This is a very cerebral book, celebrating the public man, breaking up the old mold of preconception. It is as such an enjoyable per- formance. Yet one remains convinced that there was more to Hamilton than Mitchell has been interested in showing. The great physical charm of him, the influence he made felt—these were personal, and at least partially, physical qualities. . . . However, [the author] makes amends when he presents a personal crisis, Hamilton's affair with Maria Reynolds, with compassion as well as precision." Elizabeth Stevenson
+ — N Y Her Trib Books p12 Ap 29 '62 750w

"Mitchell has traveled widely and dug deeply to find his materials. The more than 200 pages of documentation attest to the magnitude of his effort. Those footnotes, incidentally, are remarkably illuminating. Taken as a whole, this two-volume 'life' offers a learned, tightly- knit and intensely written account, not likely soon to be redone, of a seminal figure in our national history. The books exude penetrating insight, a sense of energy spent without stint, a slightly archaic idiom, a lack of concern with any scene but that which the hero occupies at a given time, and a far greater ease with ideas than with people. Perhaps it is only accidental that these are the qualities of Hamilton himself." Henry Graff
7 — + N Y Times Bk R p16 Ap 15 '62 750w

"A lengthy, detailed biography that reads often like an extended apology for its subject. This is not to deny Mitchell's study its many virtues. The treatment of Hamilton's back- ground is probably the best yet. The account of his financial program is particularly help- ful, and Mitchell does well in explaining his hero's collectivist notions." Trevor Colbourn
Sat R 45:27 Ap 21 '62 1050w

8 — + Springf'd Republican p4D My 20 '62 200w

"Professor Mitchell, who does show occa- sional signs of the 'lues Boswelliana' as Macaulay called it, has sadly to admit that Hamilton used doubtful methods to doubtful ends. However, Professor Mitchell, when he can, defends Hamilton tenaciously and often ingeniously, although one reader thinks that the criticisms of his role in the negotiations over the Jay Treaty, made by Professor Bemis a generation ago, are not refuted here. . . . This is a good book. True, it is very in- elegantly written, but at least Professor Mitchell's style is not obscure if often clumsy." + — Times [London] Lit Sup p554 Ag 3 '62 1500w

MITCHELL, FANNY TODD. Pleasures of a gourmet; il. by Peter Todd Mitchell. 166p $5.95

Arranged alphabetically by author, the *Book Review Digest* provides an evaluation of several thousand books each year.

Additionally, you could examine the *Index to Book Reviews in the Humanities* (Detroit, 1960 – date). A sample entry follows:

```
┌─────────────────────────────────────────────────────┐
│  ┌──────────────────────────────────────────┐        │
│  │ Mitchell, Broadus.  Alexander Hamilton:  The │───────── I
│  │ National Adventure, 1788-1804.              │        │
│  └──────────────────────────────────────────┘        │
│     Trevor Colbourn, 561(SatR):4/21-27               │
│    ┌──────────────────┐                              │
│    │ Robert J. Graf, Jr.│ 115:4/15-2                 │──── 2
│    └──────────────────┘                              │
│     Henry Graff, 441:4/15-16                         │
│     Louis M. Hacker,(429:)7/3-487                    │──── 3
│     R.N. Hamilton, 11:7/21-530                       │
│     John K. Hutchens, 440(4/25)27                    │──── 4
│     Elizabeth Stevenson, 440:4/29(12)                │──── 5
│     Clarence L. Ver Steeg, 395(MVHR):Sep-323         │
│     617(TLS):8/3-554                                 │
│  Mitchell, Charles.  A Fifteenth Century Italian     │
│  Plutarch.                                           │
│     Margaret Willy, 175:Autumn(61)-233               │
└─────────────────────────────────────────────────────┘
```

Fig. 31: From *Index to Book Reviews in the Humanities* 1. Author and title of book **2.** Name of reviewer **3.** Magazine or book number (a numbered list at the front of each volume of the index gives the name of the magazine or book in which the review is found) **4.** Date **5.** Page number

And you will find additional evaluation of source material in any of the following:

The Booklist. Chicago, 1905 – date.
 This work offers a selective list of new books that will meet the needs of the average public library. Annotations make it valuable for student usage.
The Reader's Adviser. Rev. and enl. by Hester R. Hoffman. 10th ed. New York, 1964.
 This work provides a systematic treatment of many books, as indicated by its subtitle: "a guide to the best in print in literature, biographies, dictionaries, encyclopedias, bibles, classics, drama, poetry, fiction, science, philosophy, travel, history."
United States Quarterly Book List. New Brunswick, N.J., 1945 – 1956.
 Critical annotations and biographies of the authors make this a valuable reference. However, you will not find recent material because it has ceased publication.

Using Primary and Secondary Sources

Whenever possible, you should make use of primary sources — that is, the original works of an author. Primary sources include novels, short stories, poems, letters, diaries, notes, manuscripts, documents, and autobiographies. Remember, an author's own words are often the most valid source of information for both direct quotation and paraphrase.

On the other hand, you should also make extensive use of articles about the subject by various authorities. These secondary sources include articles found in learned journals and book-length critical studies. However, in reading these sources, you must judge carefully the difference between fact and opinion. Just because a statement is in print does not validate it. You must learn to rely primarily on facts, and then base your own interpretations and opinions upon these. Still, if certain opinions or interpretations seem valuable to the discussion, you might wish to include them in the notes, though clearly labeled as opinion. In your later readings, perhaps, you will discover other authorities lending credence to an opinion. The weight of such evidence would then authenticate what, at first, seemed opinion.

Technique of Note Cards

As with the bibliography cards, you should be exact in recording note card information. The following system may prove helpful:

1. Write the notes legibly in ink—penciled notes become blurred because of repeated shuffling of the cards.

2. In general, use 4 x 6 cards for taking notes. The larger card distinguishes the notes from the 3 x 5 bibliography cards and provides more adequate space for writing the note.

3. Place only *one* item of information on each card. You may then shuffle and rearrange the cards during all stages of organization.

4. Since material on the back of a card may be overlooked, write on only one side of the card. However, if material should run a few lines beyond the one side on occasion, finish it on the back. But in such a situation, write "OVER" conspicuously on the face of the card.

5. Before writing the note, indicate in an abbreviated form the source of the information. Use a brief form, inasmuch as full information on the reference is available on the bibliography card. The identification may be the title of the book, the name of the author, or both. (Some students prefer a key number system, which involves numbering each bibliography entry. When a particular reference is used, this key number is then placed on the card. The danger of this technique, however, is the possibility of losing the key.)

6. Always place the proper page number at the top of each note card, since the bibliography card will not contain this specific page reference needed for a footnote entry.

7. Also, label the note card to indicate the kind of information it contains. This label at the top of the card will speed arrangement of notes with the outline.

8. Finally, write the note, using one of four basic methods: summary, précis, paraphrase, or quotation. (See below for a discussion of each method.)

Methods of Note-Taking

SUMMARY

You should write a summary note card only when the source material is of doubtful or limited importance. In other words, you probably will not use the material; yet it may somehow prove helpful later in the study. You should write, therefore, a brief sketch of the material, without great concern for style or expression. Summaries will usually lack the neatness of the other forms, although you should still take care that you make proper interpretation of the authority. Your chief purpose with the summary, as well as with the précis (see pp. 44–45) and paraphrase (see pp. 45–46), is to extract all significant facts. You must devote, at this time, sufficient energy to this task; otherwise, it will still remain to be done if you take the easy way and unthinkingly copy entire paragraphs verbatim. Also, you should remember that the summary requires a footnote when placed in the text. A sample note card follows:

```
   Theme of B.B.                    Weaver, p. 1



   Fall of Billy like fall of man--both show
   God's glory. Melv. wrote B.B. to express his
   faith: "evil is defeat" & "natural goodness
   invincible."
```

Fig. 32: Summary Note Card

Provided below is the material from which this note was drawn:

> Just as some theologians have presented the fall of man as evidence of the great glory of God, in similar manner Melville studies the evil in Claggart in vindication of the innocence of Billy Budd. For, primarily, Melville wrote *Billy Budd* in witness to his ultimate faith that evil is defeat and natural goodness invincible in the affections of man.[1]

[1]Raymond Weaver, "Introduction," *The Shorter Novels of Herman Melville* (New York, 1928), p. 1.

PRÉCIS

The précis is a very brief summary in your own words, differing from the rough summary in being more polished in style and differing from the paraphrase in being more concise. You should write the précis in complete sentences in formal English. (Only the rough summary allows abbreviations and sentence fragments.) Moreover, you must make certain that the précis is accurate in context and connotation. That is, you should preserve the essential truth of the reference material. Consequently, you will have success with the précis if you:

1. Condense the original with precision and directness. Reduce a long paragraph into a few sentences, tighten an article into a paragraph, and summarize a longer work, such as a biography, into a few pages.

2. Preserve the tone of the original. If the original is humorous, for example, maintain that tone in the précis. In the same way, retain moods of satire, exaggeration, doubt, irony, and so on.

3. Limit the use of key words or phrases from the original, and write the précis in your own language. However, retain exceptional words and phrases from the original, enclosing them in quotation marks.

4. Provide a footnote locating the source of your material.

A sample précis note card follows:

Fig. 33: Précis Note Card

```
Vere's nature         Braswell, AL, 138-139




        Centering their attention on Vere, critics
   view him either sympathetically as a man con-
   scientiously doing his duty or disapprovingly
   as a "monstrous villain" who enforces unjust
   laws that violate personal freedoms.
```

Provided below is the material from which this note was drawn:

Before going into more detail about the symbolism, however, it is necessary to analyze the role of Captain Vere, because on whatever plane one reads the novel, he is the key figure. The good-hearted Billy Budd and the evil Claggart have inspired relatively little dissent among critics: one is as inescapably good as the other is inescapably evil. The crux of the problem is what to make of their commanding officer, who alone sees and understands the situation, and yet, knowing Billy to be essentially innocent, summarily has him hanged for striking the blow that accidentally kills the master-at-arms. Most criticism of the novel treats Vere sympathetically, as a conscientious man who does his duty as he sees it. But some of the later criticism pictures him as a monstrous villain—a depraved martinet who enforces iron-clad laws regardless of whether they violate individual rights. He is charged with overweening personal ambition, hypocrisy, and the abuse of confidence.[1]

PARAPHRASE

You will probably write most of your notes in the form of paraphrase. In this type of note, you restate, in your own style, the thought or meaning expressed by another. In other words, you borrow an idea, opinion, interpretation, or statement of an authority and rewrite it in your own language. Furthermore, you write the note in about the same number of words as the original, hence the distinction between paraphrase and précis, the latter being a very *brief* summary.

Obviously, you should choose only important materials for such treatment. Material of doubtful importance should be summarized, while bulky references should be condensed with a précis. Furthermore, it is generally wiser to paraphrase material rather than to indiscriminately fill card after card with directly quoted matter. One danger of relying primarily on quoted materials is that they may lead you into plagiarism (see pp. 47–49). Of course, you are saved from plagiarism in the use of paraphrase only if you credit the thoughts you have borrowed by means of a footnote. The point of view and the presentation may be yours, but the idea, you must always remember, belongs to the original author. A sample paraphrase note card follows:

Vere compared with Pontius Pilate
              E. L. Grant Watson, NEQ, 323

      E.L. Grant Watson finds a parallel between
Captain Vere and Pontius Pilate because both
men condemn known innocents. However, Watson
praises Vere for accepting "full responsibility"
for his judgment and the consequent "bitter-
ness," unlike Pilate who washed his hands of
the execution of Jesus.

Fig. 34: Paraphrase Note Card

[1]William Braswell, *AL*, XXIX (May 1957), 138–139.

Provided below is the material from which this note was drawn:

> In Captain Vere we find a figure which may interestingly be compared to Pontius Pilate. Like Pilate, he condemns the just man to a shameful death, knowing him to be innocent, but, unlike Pilate, he does not wash his hands, but manfully assumes the full responsibility, and in such a way as to take the half, if not more than the half, of the bitterness of the execution upon himself.[1]

QUOTATION

Students frequently overuse direct quotation in taking notes, and as a result they overuse quotations in the final paper. Probably only about ten per cent of your final manuscript should appear as directly quoted matter. Therefore, you should strive, in note-taking, to limit the amount of exact transcribing of source materials. The point of research writing is to make yourself a master of your subject matter; the overuse of quotations indicates that you are not sure of yourself in this respect and are using quotations as a crutch to provide substance, or perhaps only as padding. Originality in research writing requires a personal presentation of thoroughly assimilated material. Accordingly, it should be you speaking in the major portion of your paper, giving, of course, proper credit where credit is due. You should reserve direct quotations for material that is the best evidence on the subject, that is said with especially brilliant clarity, or that is subject to refutation.

In addition, you should place quotation marks around material that is directly quoted on the note cards to distinguish it from paraphrases and the like. When thus quoting, you should copy the exact words of the author, even to the retention of any errors in the original (see "sic," p. 116). A sample note, quoting a primary source, follows:

```
Billy's nature                              Melville, 86



". . . he had none of that intuitive knowledge
of the bad which in natures not good or incom-
pletely so foreruns experience, and there-
fore may pertain, as in some instances it
too clearly does pertain, even to youth."
```

Fig. 35: Quotation Note Card[2]

[1] E. L. Grant Watson, *NEQ*, VI (June 1933), 323.

[2] Herman Melville, *Billy Budd, Sailor (An Inside Narrative)*, ed. Harrison Hayford and Merton M. Sealts, Jr. (Chicago, 1962), p. 86.

A sample note card, quoting a secondary source, follows:

```
Vere's nature              W. Y. Tindall, 73-74


"Captain Vere is faced with a dilemma.
Though he believes in Billy's innocence, naval
law and prudence alike demand punishment for
the impetuous seaman while pity and reason
counsel mercy."
```

Fig. 36: Quotation Note Card[1]

Avoiding Plagiarism

A student often unintentionally misuses his sources. Others may do so intentionally. But since you will be working with the writings of others, it is important that you learn and follow certain ethical rules as to the use of reference material. Fundamentally, plagiarism is the offering of the words or ideas of another person as one's own. Of course, the most flagrant violation is appropriating the exact words of another and offering them without documentation. But the theft is often much more subtle. The following list will suggest several forms of research writing that will constitute, in the eyes of all instructors, plagiarism:

1. The use of another's writing without proper use of quotation marks. Do not, under any circumstances, copy onto your paper a direct quotation without providing quotation marks and without crediting the source.

2. The borrowing of a phrase, the use of an idea, or the paraphrasing of material if that phrase, idea, or material is not properly introduced and documented. Also included in this category of plagiarism is the mere rearrangement of phrases from the original into a new pattern.

3. The use of another student's work. (Obviously!)

Another author's ideas, interpretations, and words are his property;

[1]William York Tindall, "The Ceremony of Innocence," in *Great Moral Dilemmas in Literature, Past and Present*, ed. R. W. McIver (New York, 1956), pp. 73–74.

they must be acknowledged as such. Consequently, you should practice the following rules of conduct when using the material of others:

1. Acknowledge borrowed material within the text by introducing the quotation or paraphrase with the name of the authority from whom it was taken.

2. Enclose within quotation marks all quoted materials.

3. Make certain that paraphrased material is written in your own style and language. The simple rearrangement of sentence patterns is unacceptable.

4. Provide a footnote for each borrowed item.

5. Provide a bibliography entry for every book or magazine that appears in the footnotes.

The examples provided below should reveal to you the difference between genuine research writing and plagiarism. First, here is an example of original reference material; it is followed by three student versions, only one of which would *not* be called plagiarism:

Original Material

> *Wuthering Heights* is the most remarkable novel in English. It is perfect, and perfect in the rarest way: it is the complete bodying forth of an intensely individual apprehension of the nature of man and life. That is to say, the content is strange enough, indeed baffling enough, while the artistic expression of it is flawless.[1]

Student Version A

```
        The most remarkable novel in English is
Wuthering Heights.  It brings forth an   indi-
vidual apprehension of the nature of man and
life; therefore it is perfect in the rarest
way.  The artistic expression is flawless, but
the content is strange, indeed baffling.
```

This piece of writing is plagiarism in its most deplorable form. The student has simply reversed the order of each sentence, retaining the essential phrasing. He provides no documentation whatever, which implies to the reader that these sentences are entirely his original creation.

[1] Walter Allen, *The English Novel* (New York, 1954), p. 223.

Student Version B

> Wuthering Heights is a great English
> novel. It is perfect in the rarest way: it
> provides an individual apprehension of man's
> nature. The artistic expression is flawless,
> although the content is strange and baffling.[1]
>
> ---
>
> [1]Walter Allen, The English Novel (New
> York, 1954), p. 223.

This student's version is also plagiarism, even though he carefully documents the citation. He has obviously copied almost directly from his source, changing only a few words and phrases. His method is neither summary nor paraphrase. This error may be avoided by direct quotation or, preferably, by a scholarly paraphrase that may include some direct quotation of any strikingly significant or well-worded ideas.

Student Version C

> Walter Allen insists that the "artistic
> expression" of Wuthering Heights is flawless.[1]
> Allen admits that the content is strange and
> even baffling, but he argues that the novel is
> perfect because it accurately presents "an in-
> tensely individual apprehension of the nature
> of man and life."[2]
>
> ---
>
> [1]Walter Allen, The English Novel (New
> York, 1954), p. 223.
> [2]Ibid.

This version represents a satisfactory handling of the source material. The authority being cited is identified and acknowledged at the outset, the substance of his comment is well expressed in the student's own language, and a key idea in the original, one strikingly worded, is directly quoted, so as to give full credit where the credit is due. The student has been wholly honest to his source, and he has made effective use of the authority for his own purposes.

V

WRITING YOUR PAPER

During the course of research, you have been making judgments and comparisons and putting details into order and completing them. You are now ready to synthesize all research materials into a paper that will give the greatest possible clarity, orderliness, and meaning to your findings. But before beginning the actual writing, you should first formulate a detailed, exact outline.

The Outline

Your rough outline should now be expanded into a clear, logical plan that will guide your paragraph development. Remember, however, that you are not bound by your original plan. If you see possibilities in a new arrangement, you should, by all means, try it.

Since you will write your final outline for your instructor and other readers, you should follow recognized conventions. First, use the standard outline symbols:

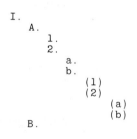

And so on. Your indentation of each heading will indicate the importance of the material; that is, you will progress from major concepts to minor ones. The degree to which you continue the subheads will depend, in part, upon the complexity of your subject; but, as a general rule, you should seldom find it necessary to carry the subheads beyond the first series of small letters.

In addition, headings of like rank on the same margin should have an equal importance. And, if you establish equal ideas, give them parallel form. Note the following:

```
I. Spring sports
   A. To play baseball
   B. Tennis
   C. Track
```

Obviously, the infinitive phrase "To play baseball" is not parallel with the nouns "Tennis" and "Track." If A is a noun, then make B and C nouns also, or if you prefer, make them all infinitives; but do not mix the grammatical forms.

When you indent outline headings, you are subordinating your ideas. Thus, if you find yourself attempting to enter a single subhead, you obviously have one major idea and not several subordinate ones. Note the following:

```
I. Spring sports
   A. Baseball
      1. History
   B. Tennis
      1. History
   C. Track
      1. History
```

Clearly, the writer intends to discuss the history of the sports. Therefore, he might rearrange the entries in the following manner:

```
              Spring Sports

       I. The History of Baseball
          A. Origin
          B. Growth
          C. Maturity
      II. The History of Tennis
```

Since a reader knows that your introduction is first and that the conclusion is last, you need not insert such labels into your outline. Instead, you should name specifically the contents of that section (see sample outlines, pp. 52, 82–83).

Because it is the main idea of the entire paper and no other idea can rank equally with it, you should not label your thesis sentence as item I in the outline. Otherwise, you may find yourself searching fruitlessly for a parallel idea to put in II, III and IV. Instead, you should write your thesis sentence separately, placing it above the outline proper.

You may write your outline in topic, sentence, or paragraph form, remembering, of course, that you cannot alternate forms within a given outline. With the topic outline, every heading is a noun or its equivalent, a gerund phrase or an infinitive phrase. With the sentence outline, every heading is a sentence or the major headings are nouns and the subheads sentences. With the paragraph outline, every heading is a paragraph or the major headings are nouns and the subheads are paragraphs; however, you will seldom use the paragraph outline, although it is valuable for papers that require multiple, complex details.

Reproduced below is a portion of the "Billy Budd" outline (see pp. 82–83 for the complete topic outline) in topic, sentence, and paragraph form:

Topic Outline

Thesis sentence: Melville uses biblical references to support his interpretation of the moral issues that govern men's lives.

I. The Bible and <u>Billy</u> <u>Budd</u>
  A. The Bible
    1. Righteousness
    2. Wickedness
  B. <u>Billy</u> <u>Budd</u>
    1. A story of man's fall
    2. A gospel story
  C. Biblical references
    1. Characters, ideas, and symbols
    2. Moral issues
      a. Ambiguities
      b. Rights and duties
II. Billy Budd and Adam

Sentence Outline

I. The Bible and <u>Billy</u> <u>Budd</u>
  A. The Bible clarifies good and evil.
    1. It praises righteousness.
    2. It condemns wickedness.
  B. Like the Bible, <u>Billy</u> <u>Budd</u> explores the realm of good and evil.
    1. Melville centers his story around the fall of man.
    2. He also writes a type of gospel story.
  C. Melville intentionally uses biblical references.
    1. He presents characters, ideas, and symbols.
    2. He thereby offers moral principles that govern our lives.
      a. He shows the ambiguities of these principles.
      b. He pictures both the rights and obligations of man.
II. Billy Budd and Adam

Paragraph Outline

I. The Bible and <u>Billy</u> <u>Budd</u>
  A. For centuries the Bible has clarified both good and evil. Its characters portray success and failure, righteousness and wickedness.
  B. <u>Billy</u> <u>Budd</u> possesses many characteristics of the Bible. Newton Arvin says that Melville bases the story on the fall of man, and Raymond Weaver calls it a gospel story.
  C. Intentionally using his biblical references, Melville distinguishes characters, ideas, and symbols. In this way, he presents the moral principles that

```
        govern our lives.  E. L. Grant Watson insists that
        Melville wishes to show the ambiguities of good and
        evil.  Certainly, the reader discovers both man's
        struggle between good and evil and the complexity of
        man's rights and duties.
   II. Billy Budd and Adam
```

Preparing to Write

If you begin writing your paper at least one full week before it is due, you should have sufficient time for writing, revising, and rewriting. However, you should not rush into the writing; instead, you should (1) examine your thesis sentence and outline to see that they provide you with a well-rounded, logically organized plan of procedure; (2) examine your tone to see that it suits your topic, purpose, and audience; and (3) examine your note cards to see that support for your ideas is abundantly supplied.

Ask yourself, "Do I know my main idea and supporting ideas?" If in doubt, you must read your thesis sentence and your outline again. With an objective eye you should examine your ideas and their logical progression through the outline. At this point you cannot afford ambiguity because each of your paragraphs must develop and expand your thesis sentence.

Next ask yourself, "Do I know my purpose?" To answer this question, you must consider both the intellectual framework (what you want the reader to understand) and the emotional framework (what you feel and what you want the reader to feel). Thus, you will have to present your material from a selected perspective that will influence your handling of the subject and your audience's reaction to it.

For example, suppose your topic deals with extremist violence in our streets. Obviously, you face an intellectual choice: you may defend or condemn the extremist groups. Complete objectivity is unlikely in a research paper which is, in fact, a form of argument. Moreover, you will determine your emotional framework by assuming either a detached or an involved position. For example, if you should select a detached approach, you would gain a degree of objectivity by giving an accurate, well-ordered presentation of both sides of the issue and by declaring your position with formal, controlled logic. If, on the other hand, you should assume an involved position, either pro or con, your presentation should be more persuasive, more demanding. You would need to avoid bias and prejudice, but you could be more subjective by condemning falsehoods, by destroying misconceptions, by rallying your audience to your cause, and by supporting your ideas with examples and comparisons that vividly portray the circumstances.

Moreover, with some topics you should consider the possibility of a humorous or a satiric approach, by which you relate, with tongue in cheek, the absurdity of a situation or you hold up to ridicule the foolishness of a condition, intending, thereby, to bring a new awareness of a problem to your reader.

Finally, ask yourself, "Do I have sufficient support from several sources for my contentions?" Since many undergraduates attempt to rely upon one major source, this question is a vital one. Remember, reliance upon the frequent use of one source is an all-too apparent confession that your research has been too restricted in its scope. The presence of almost endless strings of "Ibid." entries in your footnotes reflects a lack of industry and initiative on your part. The footnotes of your text, as well as the text itself, will reflect the quality of your research. Your instructor expects that you will put labor into collecting and assimilating adequate material from many sources and that you will then blend these sources into a readable and effective whole.

Writing Your Paper

After many hours of considerable effort, you are ready to give expression to your ideas, to share them with others, and to convince your reader of the validity of your findings. In order for your paper to reflect the care and time you have devoted to it, you must write it in the best possible language. In most instances, the reader will see only the finished product, upon which he will base his judgment of your findings and writing ability. Therefore, you should carefully construct your paragraphs, seek variety and emphasis in your sentences, and select words properly.

PARAGRAPH UNITY

You should develop only one main idea in each of your paragraphs. This rule may seem obvious; yet many students fail to follow it, expecting instead that their own mind will control the order of their presentation. Sometimes this method is successful, but most writers need exterior guidelines. The most useful guide and control of paragraph development is the topic sentence.

Appearing most often as the first sentence of your paragraph, the topic sentence points the direction of your main idea and indicates paragraph content. For example, note this sample topic sentence from the "Billy Budd" paper (pp. 80–96):

    One of Melville's first biblical comparisons is that of
    Billy Budd to Adam.

The key words of this sentence are "One . . . [comparison] . . . is . . . Billy Budd to Adam." The paragraph must develop the idea of the comparison; it may not develop an idea of other characters in the novel, such as Captain Vere or Claggart, or other biblical characters, such as Abraham or Joseph. The full paragraph, as it appears in the paper, follows:

```
      One of Melville's first biblical com-

parisons is that of Billy Budd to Adam.  Mel-

ville portrays Billy as "a sort of upright

barbarian, much such perhaps as Adam pre-

sumably might have been ere the urbane Serpent

wriggled himself into his company."4

Melville also describes him as possessing an

amiable disposition, never giving offense to

anyone.5 And, the author says that Billy

"had none of that intuitive knowledge of

the bad. . . ."6
```

By citing Melville himself, the student has developed the idea of the one comparison.

Next, compare a set of topic sentences:

```
A. Billy, like Adam, falls from grace.

B. Melville develops the fact that Billy's fall, like
   Adam's, was inevitable and unavoidable.
```

Which is a better topic sentence? Sentence A presents the idea of Billy's fall, but it is too general because it offers no direction or restriction. In contrast, Sentence B is a good topic sentence because it narrows the idea of the paragraph to the inevitability of the fall.

Look next at these topic sentences:

```
A. Melville develops a comparison of Billy and Claggart
   with David and Saul.

B. Melville develops a comparison of Billy and Claggart
   with David and Saul to reinforce a point: the
   envy of Claggart is a deeper, more pervading evil
   than Saul's.
```

There should be no doubt in your mind that Sentence B is better because it restricts the paragraph to the main idea of Claggart's envy as revealed by the comparison. A student using Sentence A as his topic sentence might eventually get to the point, but he also runs the danger of missing it entirely.

PARAGRAPH EXPANSION

Writing a good topic sentence is one thing, expanding its main idea is another. For example, suppose we have the following topic sentence:

```
Melville's allegorical treatment of Billy reveals that
man does not remain completely innocent and therefore
will fall from grace.
```

In developing the full paragraph, you could expand upon the idea of the "allegorical treatment," the "loss of innocence," or "the fall of man." In addition, you could choose any one of several rhetorical methods of paragraph development, as shown below. In other words, you may wish to write, in your notes, several rhetorical alternatives for a purpose statement, such as:

```
I will develop this topic sentence by presenting:

        a. examples of the allegorical treatment.
        b. the meaning of the term "allegorical treatment."
        c. the causes for the fall of man.
        d. the results of the fall of man.
        e. both the cause and effect of man's fall.
        f. a comparison of Billy and all other men.
```

Obviously, you have multiple opportunities for expansion of the topic sentence. Your use of illustrations will provide specific, concrete details of an abstract idea. Definition enables you to make your reader aware of what *you* mean by a term such as "allegorical treatment" or "loss of innocence." Or, if you place emphasis on a cause or an effect, you will examine the *why* of an idea. Your use of comparison enables you to distinguish between the similarities and the differences of two ideas, events, or objects.

In addition, you may add strength and structure to your argument by calling upon recognized authorities, that is, by citing the primary source (Melville) or secondary sources (those who write about Melville). Furthermore, this supporting data may also consist of statistics, tables, and graphs (see pp. 142–146) in research papers that treat such topics as "the population explosion," "germination of bacterial spores," "big city ghettoes," or "mental illness of teen-agers." Other possibilities for expansion are explication and analysis, in which case you would examine and explain, say, Melville's allegorical treatment of Billy Budd.

PARAGRAPH COHERENCE

Your attention to paragraph unity and expansion will determine, to a great extent, the coherence of your paragraph. You should so order your material that the reader will have no difficulty in following and understanding the logical progression of your ideas, from the controlling idea of your topic sentence to the complete expansion of secondary ideas. Note again this sample paragraph:

```
        One of Melville's first biblical comparisons

is that of Billy Budd to Adam.  Melville por-

trays Billy as "a sort of upright barbarian,

much such perhaps as Adam presumably might

have been ere the urbane Serpent wriggled him-

self into his company."4  Melville also de-

scribes him as possessing an amiable disposition,

never giving offense to anyone.5  And, the

author says that Billy "had none of that

intuitive knowledge of the bad. . . ."6
```

The writer achieves paragraph coherence by his maintenance of one controlling idea, Billy's comparison to Adam, and by his expansion, the citations from Melville. He gains additional coherence by repeating key words, using pronouns and synonyms, forming parallel sentence structures, and inserting transitional words and phrases (for example, *also, furthermore, nevertheless, thus,* and so on). You should use these same devices in your writing.

WRITING EFFECTIVE SENTENCES

You will achieve paragraph unity and coherence only by building effective sentences. As you write your paper, you should carefully consider your sentence syntax; that is, the relationship of words, the need for parallel structure, and the precise use of modifying phrases and clauses, as these syntactic units contribute to effective use of loose and periodic sentence patterns.

Normally, you will write the loose sentence, presenting the main clause first and gathering additions to it. Although its rambling structure prevents the emphasis gained by periodic sentences (well-proportioned sentences of several clauses), the loose sentence is natural and efficient. However, if you wish to gain sentence variety and emphasis, you should occasionally alter your normal word order or open up the sentence with modifiers, thereby delaying your main idea until the end of the sentence. That is, a periodic sentence is one in which the central meaning is delayed until the end or near the end of the sentence. As a result, your periodic sentences will suspend the reader's attention across the accumulated material. And, since the reader will subconsciously anticipate the main idea to come, you thereby bring the main idea into sharp focus. The following sentences demonstrate a few methods of building both the loose and the periodic sentence:

Participial phrase

Loose: Captain Vere becomes fond of Billy Budd, loving him as a son.

Periodic: Recognizing the essential innocence of the handsome young sailor, Captain Vere becomes fond of Billy Budd.

Adverb clause

Loose: Captain Vere becomes fond of Billy Budd when he recognizes Billy's innocent nature.

Periodic: When he recognizes Billy's innocent nature, Captain Vere becomes extremely fond of him.

Adverb

Loose: Captain Vere becomes fond of Billy Budd early in the voyage.

Periodic: Early in the voyage, Captain Vere becomes fond of Billy Budd.

Prepositional phrase

Loose: Captain Vere recognizes the young sailor's basic innocence on the day of Billy's arrival aboard the ship.

Periodic: On the first day of Billy's stay aboard the vessel, Captain Vere recognizes the young sailor's basic innocence.

Noun cluster

Loose: Captain Vere becomes fond of Billy Budd, a young, innocent sailor.

Periodic: A gentle, kind man at heart, Captain Vere becomes fond of Billy Budd.

Multiple phrases and clauses

Loose: Billy strikes Claggart a mortal blow because he needs an outlet for his terrible wrath after hearing Claggart accuse him of mutiny.

Periodic: Because he needs an outlet for his terrible wrath after hearing Claggart accuse him of mutiny, Billy strikes Claggart a mortal blow.

SUBORDINATE SENTENCE ELEMENTS

The sentences above provide examples of the multiple uses of modifying phrases and clauses. Since you need these subordinate ideas in your sentences and since they cannot stand alone, you must place them carefully so that they modify the correct word or idea. Note the following:

```
When Claggart accuses him of mutiny, Billy, suddenly
speechless, strikes Claggart with his fist.
```

The main idea, "Billy strikes Claggart," serves as the main clause, while the subordinate units, logically positioned, modify an idea in the main clause. "Suddenly speechless" modifies the subject "Billy" and "When Claggart accuses him of mutiny" modifies the verb "strikes." But notice what may happen if you forget to subordinate your minor ideas:

```
Claggart accuses Billy of mutiny, and Billy suddenly
becomes speechless. He strikes Claggart with his fist.
```

Grammatically we cannot argue with these sentences, but rhetorically we realize that the writer has given equal expression and structure to all ideas, even the minor ones. Thus, you should realize that precise handling of sentence elements requires two considerations: a recognition of your major and minor ideas and the proper placing of them within the sentence structure.

USING ACTIVE VOICE

Preferably, you should write in the active voice rather than in the passive. Note the following:

```
A. Billy Budd is called an innocent sailor by Melville.
```

```
B. Melville calls Billy Budd an innocent sailor.
```

Notice that the subject of Sentence A, "Billy Budd," receives the action, while in Sentence B the subject, "Melville," acts. Active voice is strong and dynamic; passive voice is weak because the actor is lost in a prepositional phrase or omitted altogether.

FORMING PARALLEL STRUCTURES

By recognizing ideas of equal importance and by giving them identical grammatical constructions, you can achieve a harmonious balance of words, phrases, and clauses. The creation of parallel structure will mark you as a proficient writer. Note the following:

```
Billy enters the cabin and joins Claggart in front of
Captain Vere's desk. Claggart then accuses Billy of
mutiny.
```

By joining two words into a compound structure, the writer can gain sentence balance and word economy:

```
Both Billy and Claggart stand before Captain Vere as
Claggart accuses Billy of mutiny.
```

In the next pair of sentences the writer gains balance in Sentence B by forming two equal phrases:

> A. Listening first to Claggart's accusation, Captain
>   Vere then watches Billy's violent reaction, and
>   Vere thus becomes a partner in a drama that he
>   cannot solve and cannot ignore.
>
> B. Listening first to Claggart's accusation and
>   witnessing next Billy's violent reaction, Captain
>   Vere unwillingly becomes a partner in a tragic
>   drama that he can neither escape nor resolve.

You may also gain parallelism by forming two equal clauses:

> A. Claggart accuses Billy of mutiny after trying to
>   entice him into evil because he cannot accept
>   Billy's inherent goodness.
>
> B. When he cannot entice Billy into evil and when he can
>   no longer accept Billy's inherent goodness, Claggart
>   accuses Billy of mutiny.

The balanced, periodic structure of Sentence B makes it a model of good syntactic prose form.

USING WORDS EFFECTIVELY

By carefully selecting the specific word, you will create for your reader an exact image, a clarity often absent if you use vague, general words. For example, words such as *kill, murder,* and *slay* express in abstract terms such concrete acts as *strangle, poison, drown, stab,* and *shoot to death.* Note the following:

> Billy Budd kills Claggart.

The reader, left to his own imagination, can form his own idea of the deed. But note the following version:

> With his fist, Billy Budd strikes Claggart a mortal blow.

The writer of this sentence clarifies and makes specific Billy's action. Thus, as a general rule, you should seek the specific, concrete word and avoid the vague, general one.

Also, you should avoid overworked words. Note the following sentences:

> Catch [grab, snare] the ball.
>
> Catch [overtake] that other car.
>
> Catch [hook, net, land] a fish.
>
> Catch [detect] him in the act.
>
> Catch [arrest, apprehend] the robber.

Clearly, the word *catch* is overworked. There are nine other words that could easily replace *catch* in these sentences. By referring often to a good dictionary (see p. 6), you may add variety to your word choice.

In addition, you must consider the nuances of the language. You have at your command a large supply of words, any of which might be used, but usually one word is better than another. For example, consider the word choices in the following:

$$\text{Standing} \begin{Bmatrix} \text{disdainfully} \\ \text{deceitfully} \\ \text{defiantly} \end{Bmatrix} \text{before Captain Vere, the} \begin{Bmatrix} \text{evil} \\ \text{satanic} \\ \text{crazed} \end{Bmatrix}$$

$$\text{Claggart} \begin{Bmatrix} \text{accuses} \\ \text{indicts} \\ \text{charges} \end{Bmatrix} \text{Billy Budd of} \begin{Bmatrix} \text{insurrection} \\ \text{mutiny} \\ \text{revolt} \end{Bmatrix}$$

The words in each group of synonyms have almost the same denotative value because their referents are the same or similar, but the words of each group differ slightly in connotation. Your purpose and audience should dictate your word choice.

Conversely, you will use other words that look or sound alike but that actually have distinct meanings. When doubtful about the correct usage of any of the following words, you should consult a dictionary:

accept, except	forth, fourth
adapt, adopt	imply, infer
adverse, averse	in, into
advice, advise	instance, instants
affect, effect	its, it's
allude, elude	judicial, judicious
allusion, illusion	later, latter
already, all ready	loose, lose
altogether, all together	moral, morale
almost, most	passed, past
born, borne, bourn	precede, proceed
capital, capitol	principal, principle
censor, censure	quiet, quite
cite, site, sight	respectably, respectfully,
coarse, course	respectively
complement, compliment	shone, shown
continual, continuous	statue, statute, stature
credible, credulous	than, then
desert, dessert	their, they're, there
economic, economical	threw, through
fewer, less	to, too, two
formally, formerly	who's, whose

In searching for colorful, expressive words, you may employ the simile or metaphor. Both suggest a comparison between two unlike things. The metaphor implies an analogy; for example, "Claggart is satanic" or "Claggart is a serpent." The simile expresses the comparison with the words *like, as,* or *than;* for example, "Claggart is like Satan" or

"Claggart is sly as a serpent." At the same time, however, you should avoid clichés and trite expressions, as in the following:

```
At the crack of dawn, Billy Budd stood trembling in a
cold sweat when, like a bolt from the blue, death
reared its ugly head; and Billy, not the least of those
who have gone to a watery grave, passed away into the
great beyond.
```

No less than seven clichés appear in the above sentence.

Furthermore, you should avoid pretentious, flowery language. Euphemisms, for example, may be useful to replace distasteful words, as when *passed away* is used in place of *died*. But euphemisms may also distort an idea or image, as when *bill collectors* are *adjusters*, *undertakers* are *morticians*, *jobs* are *positions*, *old folks* are *senior citizens*, the *poor* are *underprivileged* or *culturally deprived*, *sweat* is *perspiration*, *garbage* is *refuse*, the *city dump* is a *sanitary land fill*, a *depression* is a *recession*, and *janitors* are *sanitary engineers* or *building superintendents*. In short, you should strive for the exact, definitive word, realizing, however, that appropriateness may often require the more pleasant word, for example, *odor* rather than *stink*.

EMPHASIS

If you write with clarity, you should seldom need intensification. Note the following:

```
Billy himself faces the bitterest of struggles; signifi-
cantly, however, he approaches his very death with
tremendous courage.
```

Since an intelligent reader will react unfavorably to such extremism, you should guard against an abundance of intensifiers, such as *measurably, significantly, considerably, colossal, stupendous, tremendous, super,* and *very.* Simple, direct phrasing is usually more effective and meaningful, for example:

```
With an unusual serenity, Billy faces his death.
```

At the same time, you should guard against an overuse of external devices of emphasis, such as underlining, double underlining, wavy underlining, and exclamation marks.

Finally, the repetition of words is effective if used properly, as in the following:

```
Because he cannot speak, because he cannot control his
anger, because he must defend himself, Billy strikes
Claggart a mortal blow.
```

But unfortunate repetition may result in such writing as:

```
Because of a speech impediment, Billy cannot speak;
therefore, he uses his fist against Claggart instead of
speaking in his own defense.
```

In the same way, you should guard against redundancy; that is, do not repeat yourself needlessly, as in:

```
Billy is an innocent sailor who is guiltless and
blameless.
```

USING THE PROPER TENSE

Since you are dealing with an event or work of the past, your overall approach to the material should be in the past tense:

```
John Calvin was born at Noyon, Picardy, on July 10,
1509. At the age of fourteen he entered the University
of Paris and began the study of theology. He completed
his theological training at nineteen, and then as the
result of his father's wish, he went to Orleans to
study law.
```

Clearly, the use of the past tense is required with this material. But note the opening of the "Billy Budd" paper:

```
        The Bible has stood for centuries as a

    clarification of what is good and what is

    evil.  People at the center of this book

    portray success and failure, righteousness and

    wickedness.  In a striking parallel Billy Budd

    possesses many characteristics of the Bible.
```

The writer of these lines is concerned with two works of the past, but since both books continue in print, they continue into the present. Therefore, the writer uses the verbs *is, portray,* and *possesses* rather than *was, portrayed,* and *possessed.* That is, he uses the historical present tense to indicate what is true at the present time and will remain true in the future.

In the same way, you should use the present tense for most comments or observations upon events in a work under examination. Thus, in a paper on Hawthorne's *The Scarlet Letter*, instead of writing "Dimmesdale *was* weak and indecisive as he *stood* on the platform with Hester and Pearl," you would employ the present tense: "Dimmesdale *is* weak and indecisive as he *stands* on the platform. . . ." Similarly, use the present tense in referring to a view expressed by some quoted or paraphrased author, for the criticism is still in print and continues to be true in the present. Good usage demands "Professor Thompson argues," "Professor Thompson writes," or "Professor Thompson observes," rather than "Professor Thompson argued," "Professor Thompson wrote," or "Professor Thompson observed."

REVISING YOUR FIRST DRAFT

After completing the first draft, begin the revision and rewriting in a critical and exacting mood—there is no place for any complacent pride of accomplishment at this point. Conscientiously delete unnecessary material, add supporting statements and evidence, relate facts to one another, rearrange data, and rewrite. Follow this cycle until the paper meets your full approval. Check for errors in sentence structure, spelling, and punctuation, and read each quotation for accuracy. Finally, check each footnote and bibliography entry for correctness of content and form.

Handling Reference Material

As you begin transfering your note material into your written text, you may have questions about the proper use of your references. For example, you will often ask yourself, "How should I use this note—as paraphrase or quotation?" Obviously, you cannot just copy all your notes directly into the text. The trick is to skillfully incorporate a paraphrase or short quotation into your own writing so that the outside source is not obtrusive and at the same time illuminates and supports your own conclusions. You will find that this task is vital to the success of your manuscript.

SHORT PROSE QUOTATIONS AND PARAPHRASES

There are two basic forms for incorporating quoted matter into the text. First, if the quotation is no more than four lines long, you may place it within the body of the text and enclose it within quotation marks.

Suppose, for example, that you have the following material on a note card:

```
Urban growth in backward countries

R. C. Anderson, SE, XXIX, 335




"Currently, a rapid rate of urban growth is
one of the most obvious characteristics of the
underdeveloped nation."
```

There are several ways you could incorporate this material into your paper, but not all of them would be considered acceptable. Consider the following example:

Unacceptable

```
        "Currently, a rapid rate of urban growth

    is one of the most obvious characteristics of

    the underdeveloped nation."1   The farmers and

    laborers in Asia, Africa, and Latin America

    are tired of their misery.   They are moving

    to the city, hoping that things will somehow

    be better.
    _____

        1Randall C. Anderson, "The Role of Human
    Geography in the Study of Emerging Nations,"
    Social Education, XXIX (October 1965), 335.
```

This style would be unacceptable to most teachers because the writer provides no introduction for the quotation.

Acceptable

> The farmers and laborers in Asia, Africa,
> and Latin America are tired of their misery.
> They are moving to the city, hoping that
> things will somehow be better. As Randall C.
> Anderson notes, "A rapid rate of urban growth
> is one of the most obvious characteristics of
> the underdeveloped nation."[1]
>
> _____
>
> [1]"The Role of Human Geography in the
> Study of Emerging Nations," <u>Social</u> <u>Education</u>,
> XXIX (October 1965), 335.

In this example the writer has adequately introduced the quotation. Other alternatives to this version might be:

> . . . will somehow be better; the result, says Randall
> C. Anderson, is that "a rapid rate of urban growth
> is. . . ."

> . . . will somehow be better. This has led at least one
> observer to conclude that "a rapid rate of urban growth
> is. . . ."

> Randall C. Anderson points out that "a rapid rate
> of urban growth is one of the most obvious character-
> istics of the underdeveloped nation." In other words,
> farmers and laborers in Asia, Africa, and Latin America
> are moving. . . .

In the same way, your paraphrases should be properly introduced:

Acceptable

> Tired of their misery, farmers and labor-
> ers in Asia, Africa, and Latin America are
> moving to the city with hopes that things will
> somehow be better. The result, according to
> Randall C. Anderson, is a rapid urban growth
> of these underdeveloped nations.[1]
>
> _____
>
> [1]"The Role of Human Geography in the
> Study of Emerging Nations." <u>Social</u> <u>Education</u>,
> XXIX (October 1965), 335.

INTRODUCING SHORT QUOTATIONS AND PARAPHRASES

When introducing short reference material (four lines or less), you should avoid repetition of a stereotyped phrase—for example, "Professor Jones says." Rather, you should try to vary the method of formal introduction, as shown in the following:

> According to Newton Arvin, Melville centers his story around. . . .
>
> Raymond Weaver sees <u>Billy</u> <u>Budd</u> as a gospel story filled with crime, sin, punishment. . . .
>
> E. L. Grant Watson insists that Melville uses his characters to hint at. . . .
>
> Melville portrays Billy as "a sort of upright barbarian. . . ."
>
> One critic argues that "there is a mysterious justice in. . . ."
>
> Explaining Billy's tragedy, R. W. B. Lewis declares: "Fortunately, as it turned out, there had been. . . ."
>
> It was "the spirit of truth to see what needed to be done, and the spirit of faithfulness to go and do it," contends one biblical scholar.
>
> Nathalia Wright suggests that the parallel in this allusion can be. . . .
>
> Wright points out that both Billy and Vere "are subject to. . . ."
>
> The price of this social expediency, implies one authority, is a blighting, human mediocrity.

Other words that will give variety to your introductions are *accept, add, admit, affirm, believe, confirm, mention, propose, rely, report, reveal, state, submit, suggest, think,* and *verify.* However, you should avoid the monotony of such introductions by alternating them with your own contentions and with a few long single-spaced quotations (see below, "Longer Quotations," p. 70).

COMBINING PARAPHRASE AND QUOTATION

As shown above, it is a good practice to introduce your material by citing the name of the authority from which it was drawn. However, you must place a footnote index numeral at the end of paraphrased and quoted matter whether the name of the author appears in the text or not. In the following example the writer of the "Billy Budd" paper has obeyed these two rules. Additionally, he has molded into one unified paragraph both paraphrase and quotation:

> Wendell Glick provides the most logical
> answer to the moral dilemma by stressing that
> Melville deplores with Vere the injustice that
> finds Billy condemned.[28] Glick argues that
> justice to the individual, according to
> Melville's story, is not "the ultimate loyalty
> in a complex culture."[29] He states that "the
> stability of the culture has a higher claim,
> and when the two conflict, justice to the
> individual must be abrogated to keep the order
> of society intact."[30]
>
> ----------
>
> [28]"Expediency and Absolute Morality in
> Billy Budd," PMLA, LXVIII (March 1953), 104.
> [29]Ibid.
> [30]Ibid.

You cannot paraphrase and synthesize such material into the desired context without intelligent, thoughtful effort. To provide an indication of the care that is required, the writer's note card is supplied below:

> Captain Vere   Glick, p. 104
>
> "Melville sympathized with Billy Budd
> as completely as did Captain Vere. He appre-
> ciated with the Captain the stark injustice
> of a situation which finds the individual
> condemned for adherence to a standard of
> behavior most men would consider noble and
> right. But he agreed with the Captain that
> justice to the individual is not the ultimate
> loyalty in a complex culture; the stability
> of the culture has a higher claim, and when
> the two conflict, justice to the individual
> must be abrogated to keep the order of society
> intact . . . . . Melville and Captain Vere
> brought in the verdict that the claims of
> civilized society may upon occasion constitute
> a higher ethic than the claims of 'natural
> law' and personal justice."

REPRODUCING QUOTED MATERIAL

In general, you should reproduce quoted material exactly; but one exception is permitted for logical reasons: if the quotation forms a grammatical part of the sentence in which it occurs, you need not capitalize the first word of the quotation, even though it is capitalized in the original, as in:

```
Frederic I. Carpenter agrees that "the traditional
answer remains clear, but the romantic and the
idealistic have usually been confused."17
```

However, if the quotation follows a formal introduction, you should capitalize the first word as in the original:

```
Frederic I. Carpenter identifies an area of confusion
when he declares: "The traditional answer remains clear,
but the romantic and the idealistic have usually been
confused."17
```

Thus, a few rules for quoted material of four lines or less are:

1. Reproduce the quotation exactly as it appears in the original with the one exception noted above.

2. Place the material within quotation marks.

3. Insert a footnote numeral after the last word of the material.

4. Use the name of the authority, usually, to introduce the material. Items 3 and 4 apply with equal force to your paraphrases.

If your paper is based solely on a single novel or short story and if there is one footnote identifying the edition, you may employ a simpler method of documentation for citations of the primary source; that is, place the page numbers in parentheses after the prose quotations, for example:

```
Melville portrays Billy as "a sort of upright

barbarian, much such perhaps as Adam presuma-

bly might have been ere the urbane Serpent

wriggled himself into his company" (p. 52).1

Melville also describes him as possessing an

amiable disposition, never giving offense to

anyone (p. 68).
```

```
     1Citations from Melville in the text
are to Billy Budd, Sailor (An Inside Narra-
tive), ed. Harrison Hayford and Merton M.
Sealts, Jr. (Chicago, 1962).
```

LONGER QUOTATIONS

Quotations that exceed four lines should be indented and single-spaced. But do not overuse long quotations. The obvious fact is that most readers tend to skip over long single-spaced material unless it is strongly introduced and unless such quotations occur infrequently. The proper method for such quotations is shown below:

```
        Melville develops a comparison of Billy
   and Claggart with David and Saul to reinforce
   a point: the envy of Claggart is a deeper,
   more pervading evil than Saul's.  Melville
   states:

        But Claggart's was no vulgar form of the
        passion.  Nor, as directed toward Billy
        Budd, did it partake of that streak of
        apprehensive jealousy that marred Saul's
        visage perturbedly brooding on the comely
        young David.  Claggart's envy struck
        deeper.11

   So Melville wished to go farther than merely
   the parallel of jealousy in Saul and Claggart
   against. . . .
```

As indicated in this example, you should observe the following rules:

1. Do not employ quotation marks with a long quotation that is single-spaced and indented.

2. Place the footnote index numeral, as always, after the last word of the quotation.

3. Indent the material at least five spaces from the left margin and provide at least one line space both above and below the material.

4. If quoted matter begins with the opening of a paragraph, indent the first line at least ten spaces from the left margin; the quotation, that is, carries its own paragraph indentation. Otherwise there is no extra indentation of the first line.

5. Finally, make certain that the quotation is properly introduced. Use a colon to link the quotation with its introduction.

POETRY QUOTATIONS

Short passages of quoted poetry are included in the text in the following manner:

In <u>Antony</u> <u>and</u> <u>Cleopatra</u> Shakespeare states his
theme at once through the indignant, hard-
natured Roman soldier Philo, who labels Antony
"the triple pillar of the world transformed /
Into a strumpet's fool" (<u>Antony</u> I.i.12-13).
Philo thereby heralds the traditional moral
attitude of the Roman mind as opposed by the
sensuous nature of Egypt and its queen.

As this example indicates, you should again follow certain rules:

1. Set off the quotation by quotation marks.

2. Indicate two separate lines of the poetry text by the use of a virgule (/).

3. Place the documentation in parentheses immediately following the quotation.

4. Insert the documentation inside the period because the reference, like the quotation, is a part of the larger context of the sentence.

5. Omit the footnote. But be certain that the quotation is properly introduced.

6. Good scholarship requires that the edition of Shakespeare's plays, or any similar anthology, be listed in an early footnote entry, for example:

[1]Citations from Shakespeare in the text are to
<u>Shakespeare</u>: <u>Twenty-Three</u> <u>Plays</u> <u>and</u> <u>the</u> <u>Sonnets</u>, ed.
Thomas M. Parrott (New York, 1953).

Longer passages of poetry are handled differently, as shown by the following passage from Shakespeare's *Hamlet*.

In a famous soliloquy Hamlet declares:

To be, or not to be: that is the question:
Whether 't is nobler in the mind to suffer
The slings and arrows of outrageous fortune,
Or to take arms against a sea of troubles,
And by opposing end them? To die, to sleep--
No more; and by a sleep to say we end
The heart-ache and the thousand natural shocks
That flesh is heir to. . . . (<u>Ham</u>. III.i.56-63)

Also notice the form of documentation for the following:

In his poem "Among School Children," W. B. Yeats

asks two profound questions:

Are you the leaf, the blossom or the
        bole?
O body swayed to music, O brightening
        glance,
How can we know the dancer
        from the dance? (11. 62-64)

Again, you should follow certain rules:

1. Center the quotation on the page and type with single-spacing and with quotation marks omitted.

2. Use this method whenever poetry quotations run longer than two lines.

3. Place the documentation outside the final period because the reference is not a contextual part of the quoted sentence of poetry.

4. Use a colon to link the quotation with its introduction.

5. Omit the footnote. But, again, good scholarship requires an early footnote that lists the edition or anthology in which the poem is found (see 6 above).

ELLIPSIS

In a situation where less than an entire sentence of the quoted material is needed, you should use ellipsis dots to indicate omissions in the quoted material. This mark is three spaced periods, as (. . .). When the ellipsis ends a quoted passage, you should add a fourth period (or whatever punctuation is proper) to indicate the termination of thought. Note the following:

R. W. B. Lewis declares that "if Hester has sinned, she
has done so as an affirmation of life, and her sin is
the source of life. . . ."[1]

One critic insists that it is possible "to read The
Scarlet Letter . . . as an indorsement of hopeful-
ness. . . ."[1]

Phil Withim objects to the idea that "such episodes are
intended to demonstrate that Vere . . . has the intelli-
gence and insight to perceive the deeper issue."[1]

BRACKETS

You may find it necessary, on occasion, to insert personal comment within a quotation. You should enclose such an interpolation within brackets. Note the following:

> "He [Hawthorne] is concerned with the estrangement of individuals from society."

> "The black flower [of society] is shown in striking contrast to the wild rose of Nature."

> One critic indicates that "we must avoid the temptation to read it [The Scarlet Letter] heretically."

> "John F. Kennedy, assassinated in November of 1964 [sic], became overnight an immortal figure of courage and dignity in the hearts of all Americans."

Format

In its basic organization the research paper consists of the following parts:

1. One blank page
2. Title page
3. Outline (if required)
4. Body
5. Bibliography
6. One blank page

THE TITLE PAGE

The title page contains three main divisions: the title of the work, the author, and the class information. Note the following guidelines for title pages:

1. If the title requires two or more lines, position the extra line(s) in such a manner as to form an inverted pyramid.

2. Capitalize, do not underline, the title. Also, do not use a period after a centered heading.

3. Enter your own name with the word "by" directly above it.

4. Provide the class and section information and the date. Entry of the instructor's name is usually optional.

5. Employ separate lines for each item.

6. Provide balanced, two-inch margins for all sides of the title page. Remember, the primary requirement for the title page is that the material be arranged into a well-balanced page. Two examples follow:

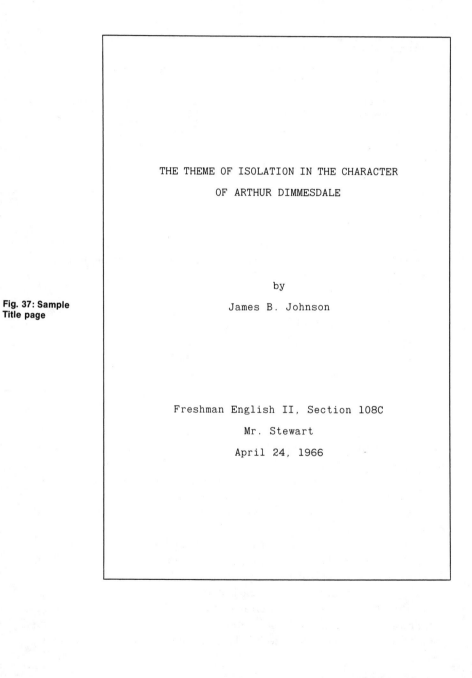

THE THEME OF ISOLATION IN THE CHARACTER

OF ARTHUR DIMMESDALE

by

James B. Johnson

**Fig. 37: Sample
Title page**

Freshman English II, Section 108C

Mr. Stewart

April 24, 1966

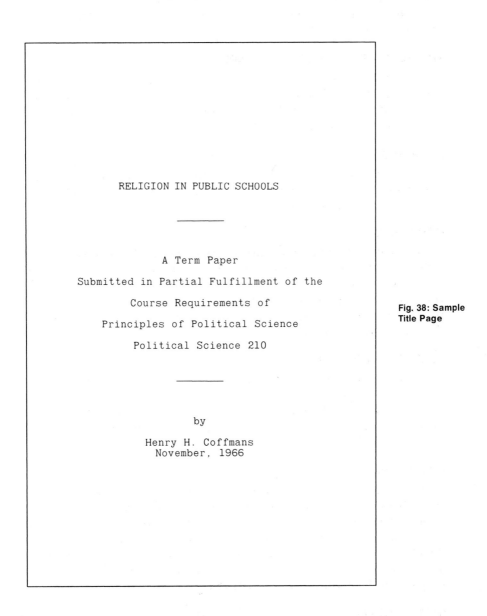

RELIGION IN PUBLIC SCHOOLS

A Term Paper
Submitted in Partial Fulfillment of the
Course Requirements of
Principles of Political Science
Political Science 210

---

by

Henry H. Coffmans
November, 1966

Fig. 38: Sample Title Page

(For another sample title page, see p. 81.)

TIIC OUTLINC

The outline follows the title page in the finished manuscript, its pages being numbered with small roman numerals (for example, iii, iv, v) in the top, right-hand corner of the page (see also "Outlining," pp. 35–39 and 50–53).

THE BODY OF THE RESEARCH PAPER

The body of the paper is obviously the most important part of your work. You should therefore be certain that your format conforms to the stipulations set forth below. (See also individual items in the "Glossary of Research Terms," pp. 139–148.)

CHAPTERS

Omit divisions altogether or separate them by subtitles or side heads (see "Subtitles" below). Divide the paper into chapters only when you have a long, complex presentation.

CONCLUSION

Normally, the final summarizing paragraph of the text will be sufficient, although special circumstances may, on occasion, demand a separate conclusion. For instance, the writer of the "Billy Budd" research paper presents a formal, five-paragraph conclusion (see pp. 92–95) in order to summarize the several comparisons between the Bible and *Billy Budd*.

FOOTNOTE NUMERALS

Place footnote numerals within the text of the paper by turning the platen of the typewriter so that the numeral strikes about half a space above the line. Each numeral immediately follows the quotation or material to which it refers (see also "Placing Footnote Numbers Within the Text," p. 99).

FOOTNOTES

Footnotes always appear on the same page as do the index numerals. Separate the footnotes from the text by placing a bar line one double-space below the text. This line, 10–15 spaces, extends from the left margin toward the center of the page. Place the footnote one double-space below the bar line. Single-space the footnotes, indent each as a paragraph, and double-space between each note. (See also "Arranging the Footnotes," pp. 99–101.)

INTRODUCTION

An introductory section is seldom necessary in the undergraduate paper; the opening paragraph(s) of the text will normally be sufficient.

However, include a separate introduction to explain unusual circumstances about an investigation.

ITALICS

Indicate italics in a typed manuscript by underlining. Always underline the title of a book, journal, or periodical, whether it appears in the text, in a footnote, or in the bibliography. Also underline publications which have a book format (for example, pamphlets, newspapers, plays, essays, long poems, and so on). In addition, underline foreign words (except proper names), quotations in a foreign language, titles of articles in a foreign language, and other foreign words not anglicized through usage. Conversely, enclose within quotation marks titles of articles, essays, chapters, sections, and short poems. Also underline words or phrases which are out of normal context or which are being emphasized.

LENGTH OF THE RESEARCH PAPER

Generally speaking, plan a paper of 2000 or 3000 words, about ten typewritten pages, excluding the title page, outline, and bibliography. However, your instructor may set definite restrictions concerning the length of the paper. Various factors make it difficult to set an arbitrary length, which may well vary with the topic, the reference material available, the time allotted to the project, and the initiative of the student.

MARGINS

The following margin requirements are recommended:

Left margin:	$1\frac{1}{2}$ inches
Right margin:	1 inch
Bottom margin:	$1\frac{1}{2}$ inches
Top margin:	$1\frac{1}{2}$ inches

Establish the top margin nine spaces below the top of a typewritten page. Place the page number seven spaces below the top of the page and in line with the right margin. However, the top margin for pages with major headings is two inches (about 14 spaces) from the top of the page.

NUMBERING

Assign a number to each page of the paper, except the blank pages. Number the paper in arabic numerals in the upper right-hand corner of the page, seven spaces down from the top edge of the page and one inch from the right edge. Number these pages consecutively from the first page of the text through the bibliography. However, do not place a number on your first page or on any other page that carries a major heading (see p. 96)—though these pages are of course counted. Number the pages before the first page of the text, except the title page, with small roman numerals, e.g., iii, iv, v, and so on, at the top, right side of the page.

PAPER

Type on one side of white bond paper, 16 or 20 pound weight, $8\frac{1}{2}$ x 11. If your final manuscript is in longhand, use ruled theme paper.

SHORT TITLES IN THE TEXT

Shorten titles mentioned often in the text after a first, full reference. For example, *English as Language: Backgrounds, Developments, Usage* should be shortened, after initial usage, to *English as Language*, both in the text and footnotes (see pp. 113–115).

SPACING

Double-space the body of the paper. However, single-space both the footnotes and bibliography, with double-spacing between each entry. Also, indent and single-space long quotations, omitting quotation marks. In addition, triple-space between a major heading and your text.

SPELLING

Spell accurately. When in doubt, always consult a dictionary. If the dictionary says a word may be spelled in two separate ways, be consistent in the form employed, as with *theatre* and *theater,* unless the variant form occurs in quoted materials. Use American spelling throughout. In addition, proofread carefully for hyphenation errors.

SUBTITLES

Rather than chapter divisions, use subtitles, centered on the page, or side heads, underlined and flush with the left margin. Both require at least one line space both above and below. Neither requires that a new page be started (see, for example, the side heads of the "Billy Budd" research paper, pp. 80–96).

TYPING

Preferably, you should submit the paper in typed form, although most instructors will accept handwritten manuscripts, if neat and legible. Also, use pica type, though the small elite face may be used if necessary. Before starting the final copy, clean the type carefully and insert a new ribbon if necessary.

PROOFREADING

You should proofread carefully after the final copy is finished, remembering that you, and you alone, are responsible for everything within the paper. Failure to proofread is an act of carelessness that may seriously lower your final grade. Typing a paper does not remove the requirement of proofreading; if anything it doubles your responsibility, whether you have done the typing yourself or had it done. Typographical errors are mistakes that will often count against the paper just as heavily as other shortcomings. Should errors be found and time does not permit retyping, you should make the necessary corrections neatly in ink. It is far better to mar a page with a few corrections than to leave damaging errors in the paper.

SAMPLE RESEARCH PAPER

AN INTERPRETATION OF MELVILLE'S

USE OF BIBLICAL CHARACTERS

IN <u>BILLY</u> <u>BUDD</u>

by

Doris Singleton

Freshman English II. Section 108B

Mr. Crampton

April 23, 1966

The comments
which follow in the
margins will serve
to clarify the form
of the research
paper and to
explain specific
problems that
the beginning
researcher may
encounter.

The title is repeated at the beginning of the outline

AN INTERPRETATION OF MELVILLE'S

USE OF BIBLICAL CHARACTERS

IN <u>BILLY BUDD</u>

OUTLINE

Preferably, the thesis sentence should be placed at the beginning of the outline.

Thesis sentence: Melville uses biblical references to support his interpretation of the moral issues that govern men's lives.

   I. The Bible and <u>Billy Budd</u>
      A. The Bible
         1. Righteousness
         2. Wickedness
      B. <u>Billy Budd</u>
         1. A story of man's fall
         2. A gospel story
      C. Biblical references
         1. Characters, ideas, and symbols
         2. Moral issues
            a. Ambiguities
            b. Rights and duties

  II. Billy Budd and Adam
      A. Melville on Billy Budd
         1. "Upright barbarian"
         2. "No cause of offense to anybody"
         3. No "intuitive knowledge of the bad"
      B. Newton Arvin on Billy Budd
         1. His "disarming good nature"
         2. His helplessness in the presence of wrong
      C. Billy's inevitable fall
         1. His defect of knowledge
         2. His stutter

 III. Saul and Claggart
      A. Claggart's envy
         1. Melville on Claggart and Saul
         2. Claggart's jealous deceit
      B. Claggart's passion
         1. Recognition of goodness
         2. Inability to share in it

  IV. Joseph and his brothers
      A. Claggart and Joseph's brothers
         1. The brothers' lie
         2. Claggart's lie
      B. Billy and Joseph
         1. Joseph's trust in God
         2. Billy's trust in Captain Vere

There is no need to index the various references placed in the outline. The student obviously has her note cards arranged to fit the outline.

V. Abraham and Isaac
   A. Vere and Abraham
      1. Abraham's obedience to God
      2. Vere's obedience to the law
   B. Loyalty to a sovereign power
      1. Spiritual necessity
      2. Social necessity

VI. Symbolic meaning of _Billy_ _Budd_
   A. Symbolism of major characters
      1. Billy's innocence
      2. Claggart's evil
      3. Vere's conscience
   B. Social expediency
      1. Justice to the individual
      2. Loyalty to society
   C. Individual morality
      1. Submission to corruption
      2. Destruction by evil
   D. Billy's death
      1. Image of crucifixion
      2. Image of man's suffering

The title is repeated
on the first page of
the body.

In lines 6-8 the
student is careful
to introduce her
quotation and
paraphrase with
the name of the
authorities.

AN INTERPRETATION OF MELVILLE'S

USE OF BIBLICAL CHARACTERS

IN BILLY BUDD

The Bible has stood for centuries as a clarification of what is good and what is evil. People at the
center of this book portray success and failure, righteousness and wickedness. In a striking parallel, Billy
Budd possesses many characteristics of the Bible. According to Newton Arvin, Melville centers his story
around the "fall of man and the loss of Paradise."[1]
Raymond Weaver sees it as a gospel story filled with
crime, sin, punishment, love, and innocence, or of vir-
tue versus vice, in which evil and horror are given
their fullest play.[2]

Throughout his tale, Melville intentionally uses
biblical references as a means of portraying and distin-
guishing various characters, ideas, and symbols, and of
presenting different moral principles by which we should
govern our lives. E. L. Grant Watson insists that Melville uses his characters to hint at a "deep and solemn

---

[1]Herman Melville: A Critical Biography (New
York, 1950), p. 294.

[2]"Introduction," The Shorter Novels of Herman
Melville (New York, 1928), p. li.

2

purpose, one no less ambitious than to portray those
ambiguities of good and evil as the mutually dependent
opposites, between which the world of realization finds
its being."[3] The reader therefore discovers, below the
surface, the struggles and passions that good and evil
involve.

As a result of the parallelism which exists between
the biblical references and his own characters, Melville
reveals hidden personality traits and the innermost
feelings of men possessed of a moral sense and aware of
their social obligations.

Billy Budd as Adam

One of Melville's first biblical comparisons is
that of Billy Budd to Adam. Melville portrays Billy as
"a sort of upright barbarian, much such perhaps as Adam
presumably might have been ere the urbane Serpent wrig-
gled himself into his company."[4] Melville also de-
scribes him as possessing an amiable disposition, never
giving offense to anyone.[5] And the author also says

---

[3]"Melville's Testament of Acceptance," NEQ,
VI (June 1933), 319-320.

[4]Herman Melville, Billy Budd, Sailor (An Inside
Narrative), ed. Harrison Hayford and Merton M. Sealts,
Jr. (Chicago, 1962), p. 52.

[5]Ibid., p. 68.

The student has
used side heads
effectively to divide
the sections of her
paper.

The organization of
each section is
excellent. The
student introduces
the comparison,
explicates the
material, and then
draws conclusions.

The footnotes run
consecutively. They
are not numbered
anew on each page.

that Billy "had none of that intuitive knowledge of the bad. . . . "[6]

Billy is thereby pictured as an innocent youth without malice or deceitfulness. He has no knowledge of the "seamy" side of life. Arvin sees Billy's goodness as "an active and disarming <u>good</u> <u>nature</u>" that wins the affection of the other sailors.[7] But Arvin stresses that the purity of Billy's innocence adds to his help-lessness in the presence of wrong.[8]

Along with this comparison, Melville develops the fact that Billy's fall, like Adam's, was inevitable and unavoidable. Both Adam and Billy are limited in their nature by a defect of knowledge. Melville provides, in Billy's stutter, a distinct symbol of his limitation. Arvin argues that "there is a mysterious justice in the fact that this stutter is his [Billy's] undoing."[9] Ex-plaining Billy's tragedy, R. W. B. Lewis declares:

> Fortunately, as it turned out, there had been a fall. Happily, there had been a sin. And, consequently, there had followed the long story of educative experience. All of that experience was at the disposal of each new

The student properly uses brackets to clarify the pronoun in the Arvin quotation.

---

[6]Melville, p. 86.

[7]<u>Herman</u> <u>Melville</u>, p. 294.

[8]Ibid.

[9]Ibid., p. 295.

member of the race. The new member inherited the corruption, but he likewise shared in wisdom. If he could never regain Adam's radical innocence, he need never regress to Adam's ignorance.[10]

Melville's allegorical treatment of Billy therefore reveals that man does not remain completely innocent and will fall. And as man benefited from the sin of Adam, so likewise, from the death of Billy the sailors learn to accept knowledge and authority, and thereby to become better men.

David and Saul

Melville develops a comparison of Billy and Claggart with David and Saul to reinforce a point: the envy of Claggart is a deeper, more pervading evil than was Saul's. Melville states:

But Claggart's was no vulgar form of the passion. Nor, as directed toward Billy Budd, did it partake of that streak of apprehensive jealousy that marred Saul's visage perturbedly brooding on the comely young David. Claggart's envy struck deeper.[11]

So Melville wished to go farther than merely the parallel of jealousy in Saul and Claggart against the handsome, innocent youths, David and Billy. Saul and Claggart cover their true feelings of hatred toward David and Billy by pretending they are extremely fond of them,

---

[10] The American Adam (Chicago, 1955), p. 73.

[11] Melville, pp. 77-78.

Long quotations are best avoided by the use of paraphrase, but the quotation by Lewis is well phrased and important to the student's argument.

A study of the section about David and Saul will reveal that the student has uncovered no secondary support for her ideas. However, she uses textual materials from the novel to develop an effective interpretation.

by directing acts of kindness toward them, and by prais-
ing them with friendly words, when in reality it is
their aim to dispose of them as quickly as possible.

Melville shows that Claggart is not jealous of
Billy as a threat to his own position aboard the ship;
rather, Claggart is jealous of Billy's innocence, which
Claggart cannot share and therefore must destroy.

Melville says that Billy has within himself a spirit that "in its simplicity never willed malice or experienced the reactionary bite of that serpent."[12] The
insight of this spirit intensified the passion of Claggart because "he saw the charm of it, the courageous
free-and-easy temper of it, and fain would have shared
it, but he despaired of it."[13]

In the analogy of Saul and David, Melville suggests
that the evil of Claggart strikes deeply into moral issues. Claggart apprehends the good in Billy, but he is
powerless to share it. Herein lies the tragedy of men
like Claggart. They cannot enjoy the good; they may
only destroy it.

Jacob and Joseph

To make Jacob believe that Joseph is dead, the
brothers kill a lamb and dip the coat in the lamb's

---

[12]Melville, p. 78.

[13]Ibid.

blood. Carrying the coat to Jacob, the brothers tell
him they could not find Joseph anywhere. One can imagine himself as the spokesman of the group of brothers
standing before Jacob deliberately lying. One would
probably ask the questions, "Will he believe me?" and
"What will he do?" One would undoubtedly have a mixture
of curiosity and apprehension as he awaits the answer.

Claggart is in this situation as he stands before
Captain Vere after accusing Billy of attempted mutiny.
Claggart is described by Melville as having "a look cur-
ious of the operation of his tactics, a look such as
might have been that of the spokesman of the envious
children of Jacob deceptively imposing upon the troubled
patriarch the blood-dyed coat of young Joseph."[14]

But the mention of Joseph and Jacob provides more
than the emotions of Claggart as he stands before Captain Vere. This allusion conveys the underlying motive
of Claggart's aggression against Billy, jealousy, which
is compared with the jealousy the other children of Jacob had for Joseph because he was the father's favorite.

Billy, like Joseph, is punished and imprisoned because of the purity of his innocence. Yet, despite this
unfair trial, Billy believes that Captain Vere is still

---

[14]Melville, p. 96.

with him, much as Joseph retained his deep-seated faith and trust that the Lord was with him. Joseph and Billy show in their controlled and innocent behavior that there is a spirit in them not present in ordinary men. It was "the spirit of truth to see what needed to be done, and the spirit of faithfulness to go and do it," contends one biblical scholar.[15]

Abraham and Isaac

To test his devotion, Abraham is commanded by God to sacrifice his son Isaac upon the altar of God. Abraham lifts the knife to kill Isaac, but God stops him. Melville alludes to this incident after Vere has virtually forced the court into finding Billy guilty. Despite a fatherly love for Billy, Vere strictly follows the law, thereby condemning Billy to death. But Melville adds this observation:

> Captain Vere in end may have developed the passion sometimes latent under an exterior stoical or indifferent. He was old enough to have been Billy's father. The austere devotee of military duty, letting himself melt back into what remains primeval in our formalized humanity, may in end have caught Billy to his heart, even as Abraham may have caught young Isaac on the brink of resolutely offering him up in obedience to the exacting behest.[16]

Captain Vere and Abraham are devoted: Abraham to God

---

[15]Cuthbert A. Simpson, "Genesis," in The Interpreter's Bible (Nashville, 1939), I, 780.

[16]Melville, p. 115.

and Vere to his military obligations. Each is willing
to sacrifice the life of someone he loves.

Nathalia Wright suggests that the parallel in this
allusion can be carried no further.[17] She observes that
"the obedience of Isaac and of Billy Budd are two different things. Isaac was not taken into Abraham's confidence any more than Abraham was taken into Jehovah's.
All is blind obedience, dependent on a jealous and ca-
pricious deity."[18] Vere is obeying the law while main-
taining sympathy for Billy Budd. There is an understanding between the two men. Billy looks to Vere for
guidance and direction, and at his death cries out, "God
bless Captain Vere!"[19] Wright points out that both
Billy and Vere "are subject to a power beyond themselves."[20] Melville never indicates what this power is.
Wright contends it is not simply evil:

> It is beyond good or evil; it is beyond con-
> flict. The realm in which Budd meets Vere is
> not the same as that in which he meets Clag-
> gart, and beyond them all is an utterly
> amoral, mysteriously influential _terra incog-
> nita_.[21]

---

[17]_Melville's Use of the Bible_ (Durham, 1949),
p. 132.

[18]Ibid.

[19]Melville, p. 123.

[20]_Melville's Use of the Bible_, p. 134.

[21]Ibid.

This paragraph is an excellent example of paraphrase and quotation of an authority.

9

Perhaps if this complex and chaotic world is to remain
in a state of peace and order, there must intervene in
our lives a sovereign loyalty which must overrule the
ordinary reservations of love and affection. The loyal-
ties to God and country deserve "all that a man can
give, and in that giving he is blessed," says Cuthbert
Simpson.[22] A spiritual and social necessity in obedience is also stressed by Simpson:

> Consider what men have done and will do for
> their clan or their country. They give their
> sons to die in battle, to "make the supreme
> sacrifice." Though they themselves are be-
> reaved, they trust that their nation may be
> blessed, because through the dedication of
> young lives the nation may hear the promise
> which was spoken to Abraham, thy seed shall
> possess the gate of his enemies.[23]

The fact that God spared Isaac and not Billy shows that
the ways of God are sometimes hidden; but ultimately,
says Simpson, "his will is found to be not contradictory
to the purest emotions planted in human souls."[24]

Conclusion

Each main character in Melville's Billy Budd is
compared in at least one way to a biblical character.
The biblical characters, by representing good and evil,

---

[22]Simpson, "Genesis," 646.

[23]Ibid.

[24]Ibid.

carry allegorical meanings. Melville uses his comparisons to suggest something hidden, something to be discovered. There are other biblical allusions in the
novel, e.g., to Jonah, Pontius Pilate, and Ananias, but
perhaps the four examined in this paper will suffice to
reveal one interpretation of Melville's meaning.

Billy Budd, as a figure of Adam, David, and Isaac,
represents an innocent person unfamiliar with evil; he
actually thinks Claggart likes him. Claggart is shown
to be representative of Satan. This view is substanti-
ated by the images of Claggart as Saul or as Joseph's
brothers. William Braswell contends that Billy represents the heart and Claggart the head.[25] He argues that
Captain Vere symbolizes the will:

> . . . he is the final authority on all matters
> aboard ship and he determines the ship's
> course of action; he has the ultimate respon-
> sibility of choosing between right and
> wrong.[26]

Braswell's comment suggests that the spiritual issue is
somehow bound by social considerations. Vere understands the injustice of the law, but Braswell states

---

[25]"Melville's Billy Budd as 'An Inside Narrative,'"
AL, XXIX (May 1957), 134-135.

[26]Braswell, additional note [1960] to "Melville's
Billy Budd as 'An Inside Narrative,'" as quoted in
William T. Stafford, Melville's Billy Budd and the
Critics (Belmont, Calif., 1961), p. 93.

Note footnote 26.
Stafford's book has
a footnote by Bras-
well that was not in-
cluded in the original
article. (See also
footnote 27 on the
following page.)

that "he sets imperfect order above anarchic dis-
order."[27]

Wendell Glick provides the most logical answer to
the dilemma by stressing that Melville deplores with
Vere the injustice that finds Billy condemned.[28] Glick
argues that justice to the individual is not "the ultimate loyalty in a complex culture," according to Melville's story.[29] He states that "the stability of the
culture has a higher claim, and when the two conflict,
justice to the individual must be abrogated to keep the
order of society intact."[30]

The stress placed by Glick upon social expediency
argues for a weakness in individual morality. Adam,
David, and Isaac must all submit to corruption or be de-
stroyed by the Claggarts in society. Individuals like
Vere must make moral judgments when innocence and corruption collide. The price of this social expediency,
implies Glick, is a blighting, human mediocrity.[31]

Billy Budd, forced to leave the Rights-of-Man, went
aboard the Bellipotent where law, not morality, is su-

_____

[27]Braswell, op. cit., 143.

[28]"Expediency and Absolute Morality in Billy Budd,"
PMLA, LXVIII (March 1953), 104.

[29]Ibid.

[30]Ibid.

[31]Ibid., 105.

Note the use of
"op. cit." in foot-
note 27. The author
directs the reader
to Braswell's
original article
(footnote 25), not
to Stafford's case-
book (see "op. cit.,"
p. 116).

preme. His death is an image of the crucifixion, but the image is not one of hope. William Braswell best summarizes the mystery of the novel by suggesting that the crucifixion, for Melville, "had long been an image of human life, more suggestive of man's suffering than of man's hope."[32]

---

[32]Braswell, 146.

There is no need to carry the final footnote to the bottom of the page. It should immediately follow the text.

Page number
omitted because of
major heading;
subsequent bibli-
ography pages
should be num-
bered in upper
right-hand corner.

Bibliography

Arvin, Newton. <u>Herman</u> <u>Melville</u>: <u>A</u> <u>Critical</u> <u>Biography</u>.
New York, 1950.

Braswell, William. "Melville's <u>Billy</u> <u>Budd</u> as 'An Inside
Narrative,'" <u>AL</u>, XXIX (May 1957), 133–146.

Glick, Wendell. "Expediency and Absolute Morality in
<u>Billy</u> <u>Budd</u>," <u>PMLA</u>, LXVIII (March 1953), 103–110.

Lewis, Richard W. B. <u>The</u> <u>American</u> <u>Adam</u>. Chicago, 1955.

Melville, Herman. <u>Billy</u> <u>Budd</u>, <u>Sailor</u> (<u>An</u> <u>Inside</u> <u>Narra-
tive</u>). Ed. Harrison Hayford and Merton M. Sealts,
Jr. Chicago, 1962.

Simpson, Cuthbert A. "Genesis," in <u>The</u> <u>Interpreter's</u>
<u>Bible</u>. 12 vols. Nashville, 1939.

Stafford, William T., ed. <u>Billy</u> <u>Budd</u> <u>and</u> <u>the</u> <u>Critics</u>.
Belmont, Calif., 1961.

Watson, E. L. Grant. "Melville's Testament of Acceptance," <u>NEQ</u>, VI (June 1933), 319–327.

Weaver, Raymond M. "Introduction," <u>The</u> <u>Shorter</u> <u>Novels</u>
<u>of</u> <u>Herman</u> <u>Melville</u>. New York, 1928.

Withim, Phil. "<u>Billy</u> <u>Budd</u>: Testament of Resistance,"
<u>MLQ</u>, XX (June 1959), 115–127.

Wright, Nathalia. <u>Melville's</u> <u>Use</u> <u>of</u> <u>the</u> <u>Bible</u>. Durham,
1949.

VI

FOOTNOTING

With as much effort as you have already exercised in organizing the body of your paper, you will now want to note your sources with complete accuracy. Consequently, you must credit in a footnote the source of every quotation, paraphrase, fact, or idea, specifying the exact location of each item so that the reader may investigate further if he so desires. Therefore, you should fully understand, perhaps even memorize, the basic forms of documentation—that is, both footnote and bibliography entries for a book and for a periodical article. (For a fuller discussion of bibliography entries, see pp. 117–130.)

The basic forms for a book are:

FOOTNOTE

> [1]Robert C. Cosbey, The Writer's Job (Glenview, Ill., 1966), p. 42.

BIBLIOGRAPHY

> Cosbey, Robert C. The Writer's Job. Glenview, Ill., 1966.

In other words, a footnote for a book differs from the bibliography entry for that book in: indentation of the footnote, raised index numeral, author's given name first, a comma following his name, publication data within parentheses, and a specific page reference.

The basic forms for periodical articles are:

FOOTNOTE

> [1]Bradford Smith, "Mark Twain and the Mystery of Identity," CE, XXIV (March 1963), 427.

BIBLIOGRAPHY

> Smith, Bradford. "Mark Twain and the Mystery of Identity," College English (March 1963), 425–430.

That is, a footnote for a periodical article differs from the bibliography entry for that article in: indentation of the footnote, raised index numeral, author's given name first, a comma following his name, the name of the journal in abbreviated form (see pp. 149–170), and a specific page reference rather than complete pagination.

You must keep your footnotes correct, clear, and concise. By recording data *carefully* and by double-checking each entry *before* typing the final manuscript, you can ensure accuracy. (Imagine the reaction of your reader, or instructor, if your reference directs him to page 568 of a book that contains only 364 pages!) Also, you must maintain clarity. Remember, for example, that "Ibid." should not appear as the first note on a page (thereby forcing the reader to turn back to the preceding page) and that "Smith, op. cit., p. 16" may confuse the reader more than a simple reference to "Smith, p. 16" (see p. 113). Finally, you should not interrupt the reader with numerous footnotes at the bottom of the page. In fact, in some cases, you can insert a brief note, within parentheses, in the text itself. Clearly, you will not seriously interrupt the reader's attention with such references in your text as (page 35), (XI, 357), or (*Ham.* III.i.56–63). Remember, however, in such cases, to write a first full reference to a work that you cite often, putting it in proper footnote position at the bottom of the page, and saying therein that subsequent references to this edition appear in your text (see pp. 70–72).

When to Footnote

Sometimes the decision to document or not to document certain information with a footnote becomes troublesome. If in doubt, you should ask yourself, "Would a mature reader be likely to know this information?" If you believe he would not, you should provide a footnote that locates the source for the reader. For example, the fact that John F. Kennedy was president of the United States would not usually require a footnote entry. Nor would you probably need to indicate a source for the fact that Kennedy made the major decisions during the Cuban missile crisis. For that matter, his decision to effect a naval blockade of Cuba is common knowledge. However, you should credit, by means of a footnote, the source of specific decisions and statements by Kennedy—for example, his communications with Khrushchev, his cabinet decisions, or his public declarations.

Naturally, you will write into your paper ideas and concepts that you have assimilated in your own mind. These thoughts may be a combination of ideas suggested by the sources or they may be an original extension of an idea found in a source. In such cases, your thoughts cannot logically be credited to any one of your sources. Therefore, a good rule of thumb might well be the following: you should footnote when borrowing directly from your notes, but you may omit the footnote when you compose sentences not directly derived from reference material. Of course, you must always footnote a quotation, précis, summary, or paraphrased sentence. (See pp. 43–47, and the discussion of plagiarism, pp. 47–49.)

In addition, you may have a tendency to construct each paragraph so that a footnote at the end of it would blanket the entire unit. But this method may result in ambiguous references. Rather, you should consider each sentence you write as a separate unit, using the rule of thumb mentioned above to assess the general nature of the material contained in it. You should not find it necessary to footnote a complete paragraph if you synthesize and develop all the material as your own. (See "Handling Reference Material," pp. 64–73.)

Placing Footnote Numbers Within the Text

The rules for inserting footnote numbers into your text are:

1. Use arabic numerals typed slightly above the line.

2. Always place the number at the *end* of your quotation, paraphrase, idea, and so on — not after introductory words or punctuation.

3. The footnote number comes immediately after the final word or punctuation — there is no space between a word or a mark of punctuation and the index numeral:

```
    Melville also describes him as possessing an
    amiable disposition, never giving offense to
    anyone.5  And the author also says that Billy
    "had none of that intuitive knowledge of the
    bad. . . ."6
```

Arranging the Footnotes

When writing your footnotes, be sure to:

1. Number the footnotes consecutively throughout the entire paper (but by chapters in longer works).

2. Collect at the bottom of each page all footnotes for citations made on that page.

3. Separate the footnotes from your text by a 12–15 space bar line, one double space below the text, extending from the left margin toward the center of the page. Double-space between this bar line and the first footnote. Also, single-space each footnote, but double-space between the notes:

---

without malice or deceitfulness. He has no

[3]E. L. Grant Watson, "Melville's Testament of Acceptance," <u>NEQ</u>, VI (June 1933), 320.

[4]R. W. B. Lewis, <u>The American Adam</u> (Chicago, 1955), p. 73.

[5]Ibid.

---

4. Do not start a footnote on one page and complete it on the next. If you will count the number of line spaces required for your footnote(s) on each page and if you make a soft pencil mark where your text should end and the footnotes begin, you will have no trouble with footnotes running off the bottom of the page. The technique is really quite simple: count the number of line spaces required for each note, add five line spaces for the one inch bottom margin, allow three line spaces to separate the text and the first footnote, and, finally, figure any line spaces to separate two or more footnotes. Thus, the three sample footnotes above would require sixteen line spaces.

5. Employ a separate line for each footnote unless you have numerous short notes. The following form is acceptable:

---

[4]Johnson, p. 3. [6]Thomas, p. 456.

[5]Ibid., p. 9. [7]Johnson, p. 9.

Also acceptable:

```
    _____

         4Johnson, p. 3.

         5Ibid., p. 9.

         6Thomas, p. 456.

         7Johnson, p. 9.
```

Footnote Form — Books

You should use the following order when placing data for books within the first, full footnote, omitting any unnecessary items:

1. The author's or authors' name(s), in normal order, followed by a comma:

> ¹Robert C. Cosbey, <u>The Writer's Job</u> (Glenview, Ill., 1966), p. 42.

Avoid abbreviations by providing the name in the fullest form known to you. Imagine the dilemma of a reader searching the card catalog for "L. Lewis" or "J. H. Smith"! However, if you supply missing ingredients — that is, ones not given on the title page of the book — place them within square brackets (for example, "L[awrence] Lewis"). In the case of well known authors — for example, "T. S. Eliot" and "Dante" — give the name in its most usual form.

2. The title of the chapter or part of the book, within quotation marks, followed by a comma inside the final quotes:

> ²Robert Penn Warren, "Blackberry Winter," <u>Reading Modern Short Stories</u>, ed. Jarvis A. Thurston (Chicago, 1955), p. 587.

This entry is usually necessary only with articles in collections or specific chapters of long reference works.

3. The title of the book, underlined, followed by a comma unless the next item is enclosed within parentheses:

> ³Robert Penn Warren, <u>Flood: A Romance of Our Time</u> (New York, 1964), p. 22.

Use the full title as shown on the title page of the book, including any subtitle (which you distinguish by a colon).

4. The name of the editor, translator, or compiler, in normal order, preceded by "ed.," "trans.," or "comp.," followed by a comma unless the next item is enclosed within parentheses:

> ⁴Olof Lagercrantz, <u>From Hell to Paradise</u>: <u>Dante and His Comedy</u>, trans. Alan Blair (New York, 1966), p. 20.

If you are discussing the editor's or translator's work rather than the text, provide his name first, followed by a comma, followed by "ed." or "trans." without further punctuation. Place the author's name, if any, preceded with "by," after the title:

> ⁵Hazelton Spencer, ed. <u>Elizabethan Plays</u> (Boston, 1933), p. 102.

> ⁶Richard Lattimore, trans. <u>The Iliad</u>, by Homer (Chicago, 1962), p. iii.

5. The edition number, if it is not the first, in arabic numerals, followed by a comma unless the next item is enclosed within parentheses:

> ⁷May Hill Arbuthnot, <u>Children and Books</u>, 3rd ed. (Chicago, 1964), p. 16.

In most cases, you will probably use and list the most recent edition, which may require such labels as "2nd ed., rev." or "4th ed., rev. and enl."

6. The series name, without quotation marks and not underlined, followed by a comma, followed by the number of this book in the series, followed by a comma unless the next item is enclosed within parentheses:

> ⁸David Fowler, <u>Piers the Plowman</u>, Univ. of Wash. Pubs. in Lang. and Lit., XVI (Seattle, 1961), p. 89.

7. The number of volumes with this title, in arabic numerals (for example "5 vols."). Use only if there is more than one volume and the information is pertinent—that is, if your reference is to the work as a whole, not to a specific passage:

> ⁹Vernon L. Parrington, <u>Main Currents in American Thought</u>, 3 vols. (New York, 1927–1932).

Note the omission of a page number in this footnote because the reference is to the entire work.

8. The place and date of publication within parentheses and with a

comma between the place and date and usually after the second paren-
thesis:

> ¹⁰Robert C. Cosbey, <u>The</u> <u>Writer's</u> <u>Job</u> (Glenview,
> Ill., 1966), p. 42.

If more than one city appears on the title page, use only the first one.
Include the name of the state if necessary for clarity (for example,
"Springfield, Mass." or "Springfield, Ill."). Do not include the name of
the publisher unless your instructor tells you to.[1] If the title page does
not carry the publication date, use the most recent copyright date as
shown on the reverse side of the title page.

9. The volume number, if the book is one of two or more volumes
with the same title, in roman numerals, followed by a comma:

> ¹¹Edgar Allan Poe, "MS. Found in a Bottle," <u>The</u>
> <u>Works</u> <u>of</u> <u>Edgar</u> <u>Allan</u> <u>Poe</u> (New York, 1903), I, 353-354.

If the volumes were published in different years, show this fact by
placing the volume number *before* the place and date of publication:

> ¹²Vernon L. Parrington, "Roger Williams,"
> <u>Main</u> <u>Currents</u> <u>in</u> <u>American</u> <u>Thought</u>, I (New York,
> 1927), 62.

10. Page number(s), preceded by a comma, in arabic numerals
unless the text has small roman numerals (for example, "p. iv."). Use
"p." and "pp." only for works of a single volume. Use complete page
references: "pp. 92–93," not "pp. 92–3"; "pp. 215–218," not
"pp. 215–8" or "pp. 215–18." Page numbers are followed by a period unless some additional information must be included (for example,
"p. 12, n. 2.").

SPECIMEN FOOTNOTES—BOOKS

Author, *first full reference*

> ¹Robert C. Cosbey, <u>The</u> <u>Writer's</u> <u>Job</u> (Glenview,
> Ill., 1966), p. 42.

Author's name already given in text

> ¹<u>The</u> <u>Writer's</u> <u>Job</u> (Glenview, Ill., 1966), p. 42.

---

[1]In which case, your note should read:

> ¹Robert C. Cosbey, <u>The</u> <u>Writer's</u> <u>Job</u> (Glenview, Ill.:
> Scott, Foresman and Company, 1966), p. 42.

Author's name and book title already given in text

¹Glenview, Ill., 1966, p. 42.

Author, *anonymous*

²The Song of Roland, trans. Frederick Bliss Lu-
quines (New York, 1960), p. 22.

Author, *anonymous but name supplied*

³[James Madison], All Impressments Unlawful and In-
admissible (Philadelphia, 1806), p. 10.

Author, *pseudonymous but name supplied*

⁴Robert Slender [Philip Freneau], Letters on Various
and Important Subjects (Philadelphia, 1799), p. 140.

Authors, *two*

⁵Cleanth Brooks and Robert Penn Warren, Understanding Poetry, 3rd ed. (New York, 1960), pp. 16–17.

Authors, *three*

⁶Wylie O. Sypherd, A. M. Fountain, and V. E. Gib-
bens, Manual of Technical Writing (Chicago, 1957),
p. 60.

Authors, *more than three*

⁷Albert C. Baugh et al., A Literary History of England (New York, 1948), p. 797, n. 11.

The use of "and others" (see p. 116) is also acceptable.

Bibles

⁸Matt. vii. 9.

Usually, you should insert this reference in the text itself, enclosed
in parentheses (see pp. 70–72). The use of the alternate form, "Matt.
7:9," is also acceptable.

Classical works

⁹Homer, The Iliad, trans. Richard Lattimore (Chicago, 1951), p. 101 (Bk. III, 11. 38–45).

¹⁰Plato, The Republic, trans. Paul Shorey (Cambridge, Mass., 1937), p. 225 (III, vi).

You should give the reader more information than the page number
for classics that appear in several editions. However, do not use this
form if you make numerous citations to one work. Rather, you
should provide an initial full reference and thereafter place the documentation in your text (see pp. 70–72).

Component part of a book

¹¹Robert Browning, "My Last Duchess," Better Reading Two: Literature, ed. Walter Blair, John Gerber, and
Eugene Garber, 4th ed. (Chicago, 1966), pp. 55–56.

Corporate authorship

[12]Commission on Education Reconstruction, <u>Organiz-</u>
<u>ing</u> <u>the</u> <u>Teaching</u> <u>Profession</u> (Glencoe, Ill., 1955), p. 3.

Use this form for a book issued in the name of an association, bureau, committee, commission, department, or society.

Edition

[13]Porter G. Perrin, <u>Writer's</u> <u>Guide</u> <u>and</u> <u>Index</u> <u>to</u>
<u>English</u>, rev. Karl W. Dykema and Wilma R. Ebbit, 4th ed.
(Chicago, 1965), pp. 416–418.

Editor

[14]Hugh Henry Brackenridge, <u>Modern</u> <u>Chivalry</u>, ed.
Claude M. Newlin (New York, 1962), p. 18.

The writer is citing Brackenridge, the author.

[15]Hardin Craig, ed. <u>The</u> <u>Complete</u> <u>Works</u> <u>of</u> <u>Shake-</u>
<u>speare</u>, rev. ed. (Chicago, 1961), p. 22.

The writer is citing Craig, the editor.

Encyclopedia

[16]H. V. Boynton, "Battle of Chattanooga," <u>The</u>
<u>Encyclopedia</u> <u>Americana</u> (1960), VI, 356–357.

Footnotes to unsigned articles begin with the title of the article.

Illustrations

See the form used with captions for illustrations, pp. 142–146.

Introduction

[17]Arnold J. Toynbee, "Introduction," <u>The</u> <u>Great</u>
<u>Frontier</u>, by Walter Prescott Webb (Austin, Texas, 1964),
p. ix.

See also below, footnote 22.

Manuscript collections

[18]British Museum, <u>Cotton</u> <u>Vitellius</u>, A. XV.

[19]Corpus Christi College, Cambridge, MS CCCC 201.

Play, *classical*

[20]Sophocles, <u>Oedipus</u> <u>the</u> <u>King</u>, in <u>The</u> <u>Complete</u>
<u>Greek</u> <u>Tragedies,</u> ed. David Grene and Richard Lattimore
(Chicago, 1959), II, 52 (ll. 977–983).

[21]William Shakespeare, <u>Macbeth</u>, in <u>Shakespeare</u>:
<u>Twenty-Three</u> <u>Plays</u> <u>and</u> <u>the</u> <u>Sonnets</u>, ed. T. M. Parrott
(New York, 1953), p. 835 (II.i.33–43).

Play, *modern*

[22]William Inge, <u>The</u> <u>Dark</u> <u>at</u> <u>the</u> <u>Top</u> <u>of</u> <u>the</u> <u>Stairs</u>,
intro. Tennessee Williams (New York, 1945), p. 87.

23Graham Greene, The Complaisant Lover (New York, 1959), p. 52 (I.ii).

> Here again, you may wish to give the reader additional information, but it is seldom necessary with modern works.

Poem, *classical*

24Dante, "Purgatorio," The Divine Comedy, trans. Lawrence Grant White (New York, 1948), p. 74 (vii. 1–12).

25Edmund Spenser, The Faerie Queen, ed. Ernest Rhys (London, 1910), I, 58–59 (I.iv.21).

> Note that this edition of *The Faerie Queen* is published in two volumes.

Poem, *modern*

26Robert Penn Warren, "Holly and Hickory," You, Emperors, and Others: Poems 1957–1960 (New York, 1960), p. 38.

27John Keats, "Ode to a Nightingale," Beginnings in Poetry, ed. William J. Martz (Chicago, 1965), pp. 90–92.

Series, *numbered*

28David Fowler, Piers the Plowman, Univ. of Wash. Pubs. in Lang. and Lit., XVI (Seattle, 1961), p. 89.

> Since a series number rather than a volume number is given, use the abbreviation "p." If there is any danger that extensive abbreviations, as used in this note, might confuse the reader, spell out the name of the series in full.

Series, *unnumbered*

29Lawrence Henry Gibson, The Coming of the Revolution: 1762–1775, ed. Henry Steele Commager and Richard B. Morris, The New American Nation Series (New York, 1954), pp. 1–10.

30Howard E. Wilson, "Education, Foreign Policy, and International Affairs," Cultural Affairs and Foreign Relations, ed. Robert Blum, The American Assembly Series (Englewood Cliffs, N.J., 1963), p. 22.

Translator

31Olof Lagercrantz, From Hell to Paradise: Dante and His Comedy, trans. Alan Blair (New York, 1966), p. 20.

> The writer is citing Lagercrantz, the author.

32Richard Lattimore, trans. The Iliad, by Homer (Chicago, 1962), p. iii.

> The writer is citing Lattimore, the translator.

Volumes, *one of several*

³³Edgar Allan Poe, "MS. Found in a Bottle," <u>The Works of Edgar Allan Poe</u> (New York, 1903), I, 353–354.

If all volumes were published in the same year, place the volume number after the facts of publication.

³⁴Christopher Marlowe, <u>The Tragical History of Doctor Faustus</u>, in <u>The Literature of England</u>, ed. George K. Anderson and William E. Buckler, 5th ed. (Chicago, 1966), I, 711.

Since *The Tragical History of Doctor Faustus* has been published separately, you may introduce the collection in which it appears with the word "in." In addition, *The Tragical History of Doctor Faustus* may be italicized or enclosed in quotation marks.

³⁵Harold Child, "Jane Austen," <u>The Cambridge History of English Literature</u>, ed. A. W. Ward and A. R. Waller, XII (London, 1914), 231–233.

Since the volumes of this work were published in different years, the volume number precedes the facts of publication. Compare notes 36 and 37.

³⁶Vernon L. Parrington, "Roger Williams," <u>Main Currents in American Thought</u>, I (New York, 1927), 62.

³⁷Bliss Perry, <u>The American Spirit in Literature</u>, in <u>The Chronicles of America Series</u>, ed. Allen Johnson, XXXIV (New Haven, 1918), 35.

Since *The American Spirit in Literature* is an entire volume, italics may be used.

Works alphabetically arranged

³⁸Edmund K. Alden in <u>DAB</u> s.v. "Alden, John."

The "s.v." is an abbreviation for *sub voce* 'under the word or heading.' This note to a familiar biographical dictionary, alphabetically arranged, eliminates the need for a long, possibly confusing reference to *The Dictionary of American Biography*, ed. Allen Johnson (New York, 1927), I, 146–147. Especially is this fact important when you consider that this work appears in several editions.

Footnote Form — Periodicals

You should use the following order when placing data within the first, full footnote, omitting any items that are unnecessary:

1. The author's name, in normal order, followed by a comma:

¹Bradford Smith, "Mark Twain and the Mystery of Identity," <u>CE</u>, XXIV (March 1963), 427.

2. The complete title of the article, enclosed within quotation marks, followed by a comma inside the second quotation mark (see footnote 1 above).

3. The name of the periodical, abbreviated according to good usage (see pp. 149–170), underlined, followed by a comma (see footnote 1 above).

4. The volume number (without the abbreviation "Vol." preceding), in capital roman numerals, followed by a comma unless the next item is enclosed within parentheses (see footnote 1 above). However, omit the volume number for weekly or monthly periodicals which are paged anew in each issue. Give instead the complete date, set off by commas, not parentheses:

> [2]Larzer Ziff, "The Other Lost Generation," <u>Sat-</u>
> <u>urday</u> <u>Review</u>, March 20, 1965, pp. 15–18.

5. The issue number or name of the issue (for example, "Spring") only when pagination of the issue is separate and the month of publication is not given:

> [3]William R. Elkins, "Thoreau's <u>Cape</u> <u>Cod</u>: The
> Violent Pond," <u>Oklahoma</u> <u>English</u> <u>Bulletin</u>, II, No. 2
> (1965), 15.

or

> [3]William R. Elkins, "Thoreau's <u>Cape</u> <u>Cod</u>: The
> Violent Pond," <u>Oklahoma</u> <u>English</u> <u>Bulletin</u>, II, Fall
> (1965), 15.
>
> The name of the journal in complete form makes this reference clear
> for the reader who may not be familiar with the *OEB*.

6. The month (if needed) and year, enclosed in parentheses, followed by a comma. If a volume covers two or more years, give only the year of the issue involved:

> [4]Robert M. Jordan, "The Non-Dramatic Disunity of
> the <u>Merchant's</u> <u>Tale</u>," <u>PMLA</u>, LXXVIII (September 1963),
> 293–294.

7. The page number(s), in arabic numerals, followed by a period, except when additional information follows (for example, "17, n."). Do not use the abbreviations "p." or "pp." except when a volume number is *not* included in the reference:

> [2]Larzer Ziff, "The Other Lost Generation," <u>Sat-</u>
> <u>urday</u> <u>Review</u>, March 20, 1965, pp. 15–18.
>
> Since a volume number is *not* included, use the abbreviation "pp."

⁴Robert M. Jordan, "The Non-Dramatic Disunity of the <u>Merchant's</u> <u>Tale</u>," <u>PMLA</u>, LXXVIII (September 1963), 293-294.

> Since a volume number is provided, do *not* use the abbreviation "pp."

SPECIMEN FOOTNOTES—PERIODICALS

¹John A. Dussinger, "Conscience and the Pattern of Christian Perfection in <u>Clarissa</u>," <u>PMLA</u>, LXXXI (June 1966), 238-239.

²Allen Austin, "T. S. Eliot's Theory of Personal Expression," <u>PMLA</u>, LXXXI (June 1966), 303, n. 3.

³Raven I. McDavid, "Sense and Nonsense About American Dialects," <u>PMLA</u>, LXXXI, No. 2 (1966)̇, 9-11.

> The issue number is provided because this issue is paged separately although it appears in the same volume of *PMLA* as the first two references.

⁴Albert Cohen, "The <u>Fantaisie</u> for Instrumental Ensemble in 17th-Century France— Its Origin and Significance," <u>MUS. Q</u>., XLVIII (March 1960), 62.

⁵Charles J. Calitri, "Love Affair with Words," rev. of Frank G. Jennings, <u>This</u> <u>Is</u> <u>Reading</u> (New York, 1965), <u>Saturday</u> <u>Review</u>, Feb. 20, 1965, p. 88.

> Note the differences in the form for a weekly periodical.

⁶Ruth Kilchenmann, "Traum und Wirklichkeit in den Werken Friedrich Schnacks," <u>GQ</u>, XXXIV (May 1961), 260-262.

⁷Allan H. Meltzer, "The Demand for Money: The Evidence from the Time Series," <u>J</u>. <u>Pol</u>. <u>Econ</u>., LXXI (June 1963), 219.

⁸Mary Mothersill, "Moral Knowledge," <u>J</u>. <u>Philos</u>., LVI (Sept. 10, 1959), 755-756.

> Since this journal is published fortnightly, yet is paged continuously through each volume, a more specific date is provided.

⁹Leonore O'Boyle, "The Democratic Left in Germany, 1848," <u>J</u>. <u>Mod</u>. <u>Hist</u>., XXXIII (December 1961), 380-381, 383.

> This page reference is clearer to the reader than "380 ff."

¹⁰Charlotte Stern, "Sayago and Sayagues in Spanish History and Literature," <u>HR</u>, XXIX (July 1961), 220.

¹¹William Thomson, "Hindemith's Contribution to Music Theory," <u>J</u>. <u>Mus</u>. <u>Theory</u>, IX, Spring (1965), 53-55.

> The issue number may be used in place of "Spring" (see item 5, p. 108).

Footnote Form — Public Documents

Since the nature of public documents is so varied, the form of the entry cannot be standardized. Therefore, common sense tells you to provide sufficient information so that the reader can easily locate the reference. Note the following:

[1]U.S., Bureau of the Budget, Special Analysis: Budget of the United States, Fiscal year 1967 (Washington, D.C., 1966), p. 2.

[2]Higher Education Act of 1965, 79 Stat. (1965).

Compare *Swain v. Alabama* below. Court cases and legislative acts follow a form stipulated by law publications. The act or case is listed first, followed by the volume number, abbreviated title, and date of the work in which the act or case is found. Also, notice that the volume number is in arabic numerals, that the date is placed within parentheses, and that a court case is italized but an act is not.

[3]Swain v. Alabama, 380 U.S. (1965).

[4]U.S., Congress, Senate, Senate Joint Resolution 1, 89th Cong., 1st sess., 1965, pp. 2–3.

[5]U.S., Congressional Record, 88th Cong., 2nd sess., 1964, CX, Part 18, 23504–23505.

[6]U.S., Constitution, Art. 2, sec. 1.

[7]U.S., Department of State, Foreign Relations of the United States: Diplomatic Papers, 1943, II, 175–177.

Compare footnote 8 below. Since the date is part of the title, it precedes the volume number.

[8]U.S., Department of State, United States Treaties and Other International Agreements, XV, Part 1, 1964, 556.

[9]U.S., Congress, House, Committee on Interstate and Foreign Commerce, Federal Cigarette Labeling and Advertising Act, 89th Cong., 1st sess., 1965, H. Rept. 449 to accompany H. R. 3014, pp. 9–12.

[10]U.S., President, "John F. Kennedy: 1963," Public Papers of the Presidents of the United States (Washington, D.C., 1964), pp. 454–455.

[11]U.S., Congress, Senate, Committee on Foreign Relations, Hearings on S. 2793, Supplemental Foreign Assistance Fiscal Year 1966—Vietnam, 89th Cong., 2nd sess., 1966, p. 8.

[12]U.S., Congress, Senate, The Constitution of the United States of America: Analysis and Interpretation, Senate Document 170, 82nd Cong., 2nd sess., 1952, pp. 512–513.

[13]U.S., Statutes at Large, LXXII, Part 1, 455.

[14]Kansas, Session Laws 1963, pp. 601–606.

Footnote Form — Other Sources

The sample entries below will enable you to determine a suitable footnote form for other types of reference material:

Bulletin

> ¹Earl French, "Personal Problems in Industrial Research and Development," Bulletin of N.Y. State School of Industrial and Labor Relations, No. 51 (October 1963), p. 22.

Dissertation, *published*

> ³Joseph Katz, <u>Plotinus' Search for the Good</u> (diss. New York, 1950), p. 15.

Dissertation, *unpublished*

> ⁴Unpubl. diss. (Princeton, 1965) by James Francis Hitchcock, "Popular Religion in Elizabethan England," p. 46.

Interview

> ⁵Interview with R. Earl Farnsworth, Principal, Northside High School, Fort Smith, Arkansas, January 4, 1966.

Leaflet

> See "Pamphlet," p. 112.

Lecture

> ⁶Charles C. Jones, "Thomas Jefferson," Lecture presented at Kansas State Teachers College, Emporia, Kansas, July 6, 1965.
>
> See also "Public Address," p. 112.

Letter, *personal*

> ⁷Information in a letter to the author from Professor David S. Berkeley of Oklahoma State University, March 6, 1966.

Mimeographed material

> ⁸Jane Smith, "Terms for the Study of Fiction" (mimeographed paper, Oklahoma City, 1965), p. 2.

Monograph

> ⁹NEA Research Division, <u>Kindergarten Practices, 1961</u> (monograph 1962-M2, Washington, D.C., 1962), p. 3.

Newspaper

[10]Editorial, <u>The Kansas City Star</u>, March 19, 1966, p. 52.

[11]Robert Speaight, "No Final Pessimism in Tragedy of Lear," <u>The Kansas City Times</u>, May 2, 1965, p. 1G.

Pamphlet

[12]William S. Ray, "Common Sense in Behavioral Research," The Institute for Child and Family Development (Greensboro, N.C., 1963), pp. 10–11.

Public address

[13]David Sarnoff, "Television: A Channel for Freedom," Address presented at the University of Detroit Academic Convocation, Detroit, 1961.

> See also "Lecture," p. 111.

Recording

[14]"Chaucer: The Nun's Priest's Tale," Caedmon recording, No. E8C40. Narrated in Middle English by Robert Ross.

[15]"I Can Hear It Now: Winston Churchill," ed. Edward R. Murrow and Fred W. Friendly, Columbia Master-works recording, No. E9C10. Narrator, Edward R. Murrow.

Report

[16]Robert Scheer, "How the United States Got Involved in Vietnam," Report presented to the Center for the Study of Democratic Institutions (Santa Barbara, Calif., 1965), pp. 66–67.

[17]Mellon Institute Research, <u>Fifty-First Annual Report</u> (Pittsburgh, 1964), pp. 6–7.

Source Books

Source books contain articles gathered from other publications and compiled into one book. These act, therefore, as a small library. If possible, you should find the original material, cite from it, and document accordingly. But when you cannot locate the primary source, cite from your source book and use the following method of footnote documentation:

[18]Cleanth Brooks, "The Formalist Critics," <u>KR</u>, XIII (1951), 73, in <u>Tolstoy and the Critics: Literature and Aesthetics</u>, ed. H. G. Duffield and Manuel Bilsky (Chicago, 1965), p. 13.

> In other words, you provide an exact reference to both books, including page numbers.

[19]Richard W. Chambers, <u>Thomas</u> <u>More</u> (New York, 1935), p. 130, in More's <u>Utopia</u> <u>and</u> <u>Its</u> <u>Critics</u>, ed. Ligeia Gallagher (Chicago, 1964), pp. 112–113.

[20]Richard Harter Fogle, <u>Hawthorne's</u> <u>Fiction</u>: <u>The</u> <u>Light</u> <u>and</u> <u>the</u> <u>Dark</u> (Norman, Okla., 1952), in <u>The</u> <u>Scarlet</u> <u>Letter</u>, ed. Sculley Bradley et al., a Norton Critical Edition (New York, 1961), p. 302.

> In this instance, the source book does not provide pagination of the original; therefore, you must omit a page reference to Fogle's book and supply a page reference to the source book only.

Television or radio program

[21]"Town Meeting of the World," C.B.S. telecast, March 1, 1966: "Nuclear Proliferation." Narrator, Eric Sevareid.

Thesis, *published*

See "Dissertation, published," p. 111.

Thesis, *unpublished*

See "Dissertation, unpublished," p. 111.

Unpublished paper

[23]William R. Elkins, "The Dream World and the Dream Vision: Meaning and Structure in Poe's Art," an unpublished paper.

Subsequent References

After you once provide full reference data for a primary citation, your subsequent notes for the same source should be brief but clear. Normally, the author's last name and the page number will suffice (for example, "Johnson, p. 12."). However, if the full first reference is not found in a recent note or if you are citing more than one book by this author, you should add the title, preferably in the shortest possible form (for example, "Johnson, *Experiences,* p. 12."). If another author has an identical surname, you must add the given name to each reference (for example, "James Johnson, p. 12.").

As an alternative to repeating the title or author's name, you may use the Latinate abbreviation "Ibid." ('in the same place') *if* it refers to the source in the immediately preceding footnote and *if* it appears on the same page. For example, when you refer to the identical page(s) of the preceding note, insert only "Ibid.," capitalized and followed by a period ("Ibid."). If your reference is to the same book as the preceding note but to a different page, insert "Ibid.," followed by a comma, followed by the page number ("Ibid., p. 16.").

You should find it unnecessary to employ the Latinate abbreviations "op. cit." and "loc. cit." "Op. cit." is an abbreviation for *opere citato*, which means 'in the work cited.' It is sometimes employed when nonconsecutive references are made to the same work (for example, "Jones, op. cit., p. 65."). But a simple reference to "Jones, p. 65" serves the same purpose and is less confusing. "Loc. cit." is an abbreviation for *loco citato*, which means 'in the place cited.' Since this footnote names the exact source listed immediately preceding it, the author's name and a page reference are omitted (for example, "Loc. cit."). But the use of "Ibid." without a page reference serves the same purpose (see above).

Note the following sequence of specimen footnotes:

¹Meyer H. Abrams, The Mirror and the Lamp (New York, 1953), p. 33.

²Ibid., p. 35.

But do not use this form if it occurs on a different page.

³Laurence Perrine, Sound and Sense: An Introduction to Poetry (New York, 1963), p. 45.

⁴New York, 1964, p. 22.

This note refers to William W. Watt, *An American Rhetoric*; but, in this instance, both the author and title have been mentioned in the text (see p. 104). Compare footnote 7.

⁵Perrine, p. 12.

⁶Abrams, p. 36.

⁷Watt, An American Rhetoric, p. 22.

Same source as footnote 4, but you must now clarify the note by providing the author and title since neither is mentioned in the text.

⁸Ibid.

But use only on the same page with footnote 7.

⁹Ibid., p. 29.

But use only on the same page with footnotes 7 and 8.

¹⁰Laurence Perrine, Story and Structure, 2nd ed. (New York, 1966), p. 4.

¹¹Wendell Glick, "Expediency and Absolute Morality in Billy Budd," PMLA, LXVIII (March 1953), 104.

¹²Perrine, Sound and Sense, p. 124.

Since two books by Perrine appear above, you must add a title to this note.

¹³Glick, 104; cf. William Braswell, "Melville's Billy Budd as 'An Inside Narrative,'" AL, XXIX (May 1957), 133–146.

¹⁴Glick, 108.

"Ibid., 108" would, perhaps, confuse the reader.

¹⁵Raven I. McDavid, "Sense and Nonsense About American Dialects," PMLA, LXXXI, No. 2 (1966), 10.

¹⁶Watt, An American Rhetoric, p. 30.

If this note appears several pages beyond footnote 7, you extend common courtesy by adding the title.

¹⁷Ibid., p. 32; cf. McDavid, 11.

¹⁸See, e.g., Allen Austin, "T. S. Eliot's Theory of Personal Expression," PMLA, LXXXI (June 1966), 303.

¹⁹Watt, p. 31.

Content Footnotes

As shown on the preceding pages, reference footnotes perform the basic function of documenting the original source. But you may have occasion to write other types of notes, classified as content footnotes, offering further information that the average reader might need or profit by. Rather than distract the reader with an incidentally related item within the text, you should place it within a footnote, using one of the following types of content footnotes:

Definition

¹Briefly, existentialism expounds the theory that man lives in a purposeless universe in which he must exercise freedom of will to combat his environment.

This type of note defines or amplifies a term or phrase you have used in the text.

Explanation and Elaboration

²Jean-Paul Sartre became the chief spokesman for existentialism in France after World War II. (Smith, p. 6.)

This note offers additional information that is not pertinent to textual matters. The entry at the end is necessary if the information is borrowed from an authority.

Evaluation and Comparison of Authorities

³Cf. Edmund Wilson, Axel's Castle, p. 114: "As a critic, Eliot occupies today a position of distinction and influence equal in importance to his position as a poet."

The writer is asking the reader to compare textual analysis with Wilson's statement.

Cross Reference to Another Part of the Paper

⁴The importance of Emerson as a poet, however, is questioned by some authorities. See above, p. 3.

The writer is asking the reader to refer to an earlier portion of the paper for the discussion of Emerson.

Abbreviations in Footnotes

You should employ abbreviations often and consistently in the footnotes, though in your text you should avoid them (except "Dr.," "Esq.," "Hon.," "Jr.," "Mr.," "Mrs.," "Rev.," and "St." In footnotes you should abbreviate dates (for example, "Jan.," "Feb."), institutions (for example, "Dept.," "Assn."), and publications (for example, "J.," "Jour.," "diss."). In addition, you may abbreviate many well-known periodicals by listing only the initials (for example, "*CE*," "*MLN*"; see p. 157). Finally, you may use or encounter the following common abbreviations and reference words:

A.D. *anno Domini* 'in the year of the Lord'; precedes numerals with no space between letters, as in "A.D. 350"

anon. anonymous

art., arts. article(s)

B.C. 'Before Christ'; follows numerals with no space between letters, as in "500 B.C."

bk., bks. book(s)

ca. (*or* c.) *circa* 'about,' used to indicate an approximate date, as in "ca. 1812"

cf. *confer* 'compare' (one source with another); not, however, to be used in place of "see"

ch., chs. (*or* chap., chaps.) chapter(s)

col., cols. column(s)

comp. compiled (by) or compiler

diss. dissertation

ed., eds. editor(s), edition, or edited (by)

e.g. *exempli gratia* 'for example,' preceded and followed by a comma

enl. enlarged, as in "enl. ed."

esp. especially, as in "pp. 312–315, esp. p. 313"

et al. *et alii* 'and others'; "John Smith et al." means John Smith and other authors.

et pas. *et passim* 'here and there' (see "passim")

et seq. *et sequens* 'and the following'; "pp. 9 et seq.' means page nine and the following page; compare "f." and "ff."

f., ff. page or pages following a given page; "pp. 8 f." means page eight and the following page; but exact references are preferable, for example, "pp. 45–51, 55, 58" instead of "pp. 45 ff."

ibid. *ibidem* 'in the same place,' i.e., in the immediately preceding title (see p. 113).

i.e. *id est* 'that is,' preceded and followed by a comma

illus. illustrated by, illustrations, or illustrator

infra 'below,' refers to a succeeding portion of the text; compare "supra." Generally, it is best to write "see below"

intro. (*or* introd.) introduction (by)

l., ll. line(s)

loc. cit. *loco citato* 'in the place (passage) cited' (see p. 114)

MS, MSS manuscript(s); but followed by a period ("MS.") when referring to a specific manuscript

n., nn. note(s), as "p. 23, n. 2" or "p. 51 n."

n.d. no date (in a book's title or copyright pages)

no., nos. number(s)

n.p. no place (of publication)

op. cit. *opere citato* 'in the work cited' (see p. 114)

p., pp. page(s)

passim 'here and there throughout the work,' e.g., "pp. 67, 72, et passim"; cf. "f." and "ff."

pseud. pseudonym

pt., pts. part(s)

rev. revised (by), revision, review, or reviewed (by)

sec., secs. section(s)

sic 'thus,' placed in brackets to indicate that an error has been made in the quoted passage and that the writer is quoting accurately

sup. (*or* supra) 'above,' refers to a preceding portion of the text; it is just as easy to write "above," however

s.v. *sub voce (verbo)* 'under the word or heading' (see p. 107)

trans. (*or* tr.) translator, translated (by), or translation

vol., vols. volume(s), as in "Vol. III"

VII

THE BIBLIOGRAPHY

After writing your paper, you should prepare a selected bibliography, listing only the source material actually used in the writing of your manuscript. That is, you should provide publication data for each reference. In fact, some instructors may request that you label the bibliography "List of References Cited." In other words, the bibliography will offer the reader a limited indication of the scholarship related to your subject.

If you have carefully developed your working bibliography (pp. 9–14), you will find that preparation of the final one is a relatively simple process. In fact, the final bibliography is not a new assignment because your bibliography cards, arranged alphabetically, already provide the necessary information. However, this fact will be true only if you have kept the bibliography cards up-to-date during note-taking by adding new sources and by disposing of cards that you have found to be irrelevant.

To repeat: you should include in the bibliography all works actually used in your study. And you must, without exception, include a bibliography entry for all first references in the footnotes. You may also insert other works pertinent to the paper, but do not include books that were of no value in the research, even though you investigated them.

Bibliography Form

You should arrange the items of the bibliography in alphabetical order by the surname of the author. Place the first line of each entry flush with the left margin and indent succeeding lines approximately five spaces. Single-space each entry, but double-space between each reference. Study carefully the examples given in the following sample "Selected Bibliography":

A SELECTED BIBLIOGRAPHY

Catford, J. C. "Phonology and the Teaching of Pronunciation," <u>College English</u>, XXVII (May 1966), 605–613.

Chayes, Irene H. "Rhetoric as Drama: An Approach to the Romantic Ode," <u>PMLA</u>, LXXIX (March 1964), 67–79.

Ciardi, John, trans. <u>The Purgatorio</u>, by Dante. New York, 1961.

Cohen, B. Bernard. <u>Literature for Understanding</u>. Chicago, 1966.

——————— . <u>Writing About Literature</u>. Chicago, 1963.

Cosbey, Robert C. <u>The Writer's Job</u>. Glenview, Ill., 1966.

Craig, Hardin, ed. <u>The Complete Works of Shake-speare</u>. Rev. ed. Chicago, 1961.

Lagercrantz, Olof. <u>From Hell to Paradise: Dante and His Comedy</u>, trans. Alan Blair. New York, 1966.

Fig.39: Sample Bibliography Page

BIBLIOGRAPHY FORM—BOOKS

When entering references to books, you should use the following order, omitting unnecessary items:

1. The author's name, surname first, followed by given name or initials, followed by a period:

Cosbey, Robert C. <u>The Writer's Job</u>. Glenview, Ill., 1966.

Always give authors' names in the fullest possible form; for example, "Cosbey, Robert C." rather than "Cosbey, R. C." unless, as indicated on the title page of the book, the author's preference is for initials.

However, if an author has two or more works in the bibliography, do not repeat his name with each work. Rather, insert a continuous, twelve-space line flush with the left margin, followed by a period:

```
Cohen, B. Bernard.  Literature for Understanding.  Chi-
     cago, 1966.

-------------. Writing About Literature.  Chicago, 1963.
```

An alternative is that of extending the line of dashes as long or as
short as the author's name.

2. A chapter or a part of a book, placed before the title, within
quotation marks or underlined, followed by a comma, followed by the
word "in" and the title:

```
Aristophanes.  The Birds, in Five Comedies of Aristoph-
     anes, trans. Benjamin B. Rogers.  Garden City,
     N.Y., 1955.
```

This distinction of chapter or part of a book is not usually made in
bibliographies except when the work is separately edited, translated, or
written. For example, note the following footnote:

```
35Harold Child, "Jane Austen," The Cambridge
History of English Literature, ed. A. W. Ward and A. R.
Waller, XII (London, 1932), 231-233.
```

Since "Jane Austen" is *not* a separately published work, your bibliography entry may read:

```
Ward, A. W., and A. R. Waller, eds. The Cambridge
     History of English Literature.  15 vols. London,
     1932.
```

However, if you (or your instructor) prefer a more complete entry, use
the following form:

```
Child, Harold.  "Jane Austen," in The Cambridge History
     of English Literature, ed.  A. W.  Ward and A. R.
     Waller.  London, 1932, XII, 231-244.
```

3. The title of the work, underlined, followed by a period:

```
Warren, Robert Penn.  Flood: A Romance of Our Time.  New
     York, 1964.
```

4. The name of the editor or translator, preceded by a comma and
"ed." or "trans." without further punctuation:

```
Lagercrantz, Olof.  From Hell to Paradise: Dante and His
     Comedy, trans. Alan Blair.  New York, 1966.
```

However, if the work is a collection or if the editor's or translator's work rather than the text is under discussion, place the editor's or translator's name first, followed by a comma, followed by "ed." or "eds." or "trans." without further punctuation:

```
Schmidt, Dolores Barracano, and Earl Robert Schmidt,
     eds. The Deputy Reader: Studies in Moral Respon-
     sibility. Chicago, 1965.

Craig, Hardin, ed. The Complete Works of Shakespeare.
     Rev. ed. Chicago, 1961.

Ciardi, John, trans. The Purgatorio, by Dante. New
     York, 1961.
```

5. Edition used, whenever it is not the first, in arabic numerals (for example, "2nd ed."), without further punctuation:

```
Arbuthnot, May Hill. Children and Books. 3rd ed. Chi-
     cago, 1964.
```

6. The name of the series, without quotation marks and not underlined, followed by a comma, followed by the number of this work in the series (for example, "VII," or "Vol. III," or "No. 2"), followed by a period:

```
Fowler, David. Piers the Plowman. University of Wash-
     ington Publications in Language and Literature,
     XVI. Seattle, 1961.
```

7. The number of volumes with this particular title, if more than one, in arabic numerals (for example, "6 vols."):

```
Parrington, Vernon L. Main Currents in American Thought.
     3 vols. New York, 1927–1932.
```
Note that the volumes were not published in the same year.

8. The place and date of publication, followed by a period (for example, "New York, 1967.").[1] Whenever more than one place of publication appears on the title page, the first city mentioned is usually sufficient. Also, if successive dates of copyright are given, the most recent is usually sufficient (unless your study is specifically concerned with an earlier edition):

```
Steinbeck, John. The Grapes of Wrath. New York, 1939.
```

[1]Some instructors may request that you include the name of the publisher (for example, "Cosbey, Robert C. *The Writer's Job.* Glenview, Illinois: Scott, Foresman and Company, 1966."). In this form, a colon follows the place of publication, followed by the name of the publisher, followed by a comma and the date of publication, ending with a period.

Include the name of the state if necessary for clarity:

> Blum, Robert, ed. <u>Cultural</u> <u>Affairs</u> <u>and</u> <u>Foreign</u> <u>Rela-</u>
> <u>tions</u>. The American Assembly Series. Englewood
> Cliffs, N.J., 1963.

If the place or date of publication is not provided, insert either "n.p." or "n.d.":

> Venturi, Lionello. <u>Botticelli</u>. With 50 Plates, Green-
> wich, Conn., n.d.

> Lowell, James Russell. <u>Democracy</u>. N.p., 1886.

9. The volume number, in capital roman numerals, preceded and followed by a comma, only if you find it necessary to specify such information (and the occasions are rare because you will normally insert only the total number of volumes, for example, "5 vols."). Remember that your footnote contains the specific location of the material:

> Child, Harold. "Jane Austen," in <u>The</u> <u>Cambridge</u> <u>History</u>
> <u>of</u> <u>English</u> <u>Literature</u>, ed. A. W. Ward and A. R.
> Waller. London, 1932, XII, 231–244.

10. Page numbers of the entire selection, in arabic numerals, preceded by a comma and followed by a period. Again, supply this information only upon rare occasions (see item 9 above and item 2, p. 119).

Sample Bibliography Entries — Books

Author

> Cosbey, Robert C. <u>The</u> <u>Writer's</u> <u>Job</u>. Glenview, Ill.,
> 1966.

Author, *anonymous*

> <u>The</u> <u>Song</u> <u>of</u> <u>Roland</u>, trans. Frederick Bliss Luquines.
> New York, 1960.
>
> > Usually, you should alphabetize this entry by the "S" of the first important word of the title, but alphabetizing by the "T" is also a common practice.

Author, *anonymous but name supplied*

> [Madison, James.] <u>All</u> <u>Impressments</u> <u>Unlawful</u> <u>and</u> <u>Inad-</u>
> <u>missible</u>. Philadelphia, 1806.

Author, *pseudonymous but name supplied*

> Slender, Robert [Freneau, Philip]. <u>Letters</u> <u>on</u> <u>Various</u>
> <u>and</u> <u>Important</u> <u>Subjects</u>. Philadelphia, 1799.

Author, *more than one work by the same author*

> Behrman, S[amuel] N[athaniel]. <u>Rain From Heaven</u>. New
> York, 1935.
>
> ——————————. <u>Wine of Choice</u>. New York, 1938.
>
>> Rather than repeat the author's name in succeeding entries, insert
>> 12 continuous typewriter dashes, above the line. Another common
>> practice is that of extending the line of dashes as long or as short
>> as the author's name. Also, note that material not listed on the title
>> page that you insert into the entry should be enclosed in brackets.

Authors, *two*

> Brooks, Cleanth, and Robert Penn Warren. <u>Understanding
> Poetry</u>. 3rd ed. New York, 1960.
>
>> Although the first author's name is inverted, the other's is not.

Authors, *three*

> Sypherd, Wylie O., A. M. Fountain, and V. E. Gibbens.
> <u>Manual of Technical Writing</u>. Chicago, 1957.

Authors, *more than three*

> Baugh, Albert C., Tucker Brooke, Samuel C. Chew, Kemp
> Malone, and George Sherburn. <u>A Literary History of
> England</u>. New York, 1948.
>
>> An alternative to this form is the use of "et al." or "and others," as
>> follows:
>
> Baugh, Albert C., et al. <u>A Literary History of England</u>.
> New York, 1948.

Bibles

> The Bible.
>
> The Bible. Revised Standard Version.
>
>> The King James Version is assumed unless you specify another
>> version.

Classical works

> Homer. <u>The Iliad</u>, trans. Richard Lattimore. Chicago,
> 1951.
>
> Shorey, Paul, trans. <u>The Republic</u>, by Plato. Cambridge,
> Mass., 1937.
>
>> Use the translator's name first if his work rather than the text is under
>> discussion (see p. 120).

Component part of a book

> Aristophanes. <u>The Birds</u>, in <u>Five Comedies of Aristoph-
> anes</u>, trans. Benjamin B. Rogers. Garden City,
> N.Y., 1955.
>
>> See item 2, p. 119.

Corporate authorship

> Bureau of National Affairs. <u>The</u> <u>New</u> <u>Wage</u> <u>and</u> <u>Hour</u> <u>Law</u>. Washington, D.C., 1961.

Encyclopedia

> Boynton, H. V. "Battle of Chattanooga," <u>The</u> <u>Encyclo-</u> <u>pedia</u> <u>Americana</u> (1960), VI, 356–359.
>
> If the article is unsigned, begin the entry with the title of the article.

Edition

> Arbuthnot, May Hill. <u>Children</u> <u>and</u> <u>Books</u>. 3rd ed. Chicago, 1964.
>
> Perrin, Porter G. <u>Writer's</u> <u>Guide</u> <u>and</u> <u>Index</u> <u>to</u> <u>English</u>, rev. Karl W. Dykema and Wilma R. Ebbit. 4th ed. Chicago, 1965.

Editor

> Shackford, James Atkins. <u>David</u> <u>Crockett</u>: <u>The</u> <u>Man</u> <u>and</u> <u>the</u> <u>Legend</u>, ed. John B. Shackford. Chapel Hill, N.C., 1956.
>
> Craig, Hardin, ed. <u>The</u> <u>Complete</u> <u>Works</u> <u>of</u> <u>Shakespeare</u>. Rev. ed. Chicago, 1961.
>
> If the work is a collection or if the editor's work rather than the text is under discussion, place the editor's name first (see item 4, pp. 119– 120).

Illustrations

> Venturi, Lionello. <u>Botticelli</u>. With 50 Plates. Greenwich, Conn., n.d.
>
> Honoré <u>Daumier</u>: <u>Drawings</u> <u>and</u> <u>Watercolours</u>, selected and with introduction by Jean Adhémar. With 58 Illustrations. New York, 1954.

Introduction

> Webb, Walter Prescott. <u>The</u> <u>Great</u> <u>Frontier</u>, introduction by Arnold J. Toynbee. Austin, Texas, 1964.

Manuscript collections

> British Museum. <u>Cotton</u> <u>Vitellius</u>, A. XV.
>
> Corpus Christi College, Cambridge. MS CCCC 201.

Play, *classical*

> Shakespeare, William. <u>Macbeth</u>, in <u>Shakespeare</u>: <u>Twenty-</u> <u>Three</u> <u>Plays</u> <u>and</u> <u>the</u> <u>Sonnets</u>, ed. T. M. Parrott. New York, 1953.
>
> or
>
> Parrott, T. M., ed. <u>Shakespeare</u>: <u>Twenty</u>–<u>Three</u> <u>Plays</u> <u>and</u> <u>the</u> <u>Sonnets</u>. New York, 1953.
>
> See item 2, p. 119, and item 4, pp. 119–120.

Play, *modern*

> Greene, Graham. The Complaisant Lover. New York, 1959.

Poem, *classical*

> Dante. The Divine Comedy. trans. Lawrence Grant White. New York, 1948.
>
> Ciardi, John, trans. The Purgatorio, by Dante. New York, 1961.
>> Use the translator's name first if his work rather than the text is under discussion (see p. 120).

Poem, *modern*

> Warren, Robert Penn. You, Emperors, and Others: Poems 1957–1960. New York, 1960.
>
> Keats, John. "Ode to a Nightingale," in Beginnings in Poetry, ed. William J. Martz. Chicago, 1965.

Series, *numbered and unnumbered*

> Fowler, David. Piers the Plowman. University of Washington Publications in Language and Literature, XVI. Seattle, 1961.
>
> Gibson, Lawrence Henry. The Coming of the Revolution: 1763–1775, ed. Henry Steele Commager and Richard B. Morris. The New American Nation Series. New York, 1954.

Series, *paperback*

> Commager, Henry Steele. The Nature and the Study of History, ed. Raymond H. Muessig and Vincent R. Rogers. Social Science Seminar Series. Columbus, Ohio, 1965.
>
> Wilson, Howard E. "Education, Foreign Policy, and International Relations," in Cultural Affairs and Foreign Relations, ed. Robert Blum. The American Assembly Series. Englewood Cliffs, N.J., 1963.

or

> Blum, Robert, ed. Cultural Affairs and Foreign Relations. The American Assembly Series. Englewood Cliffs, N.J., 1963.
>> Preferably, use the latter form; see item 2, p. 119, and item 6, p. 120.

Translator

> Lagercrantz, Olof. From Hell to Paradise: Dante and His Comedy, trans. Alan Blair. New York, 1966.
>
> Ciardi, John, trans. The Purgatorio, by Dante. New York, 1961.
>> If the translator's work rather than the text is under discussion, place the translator's name first (see item 4, pp. 119–120).

Volumes, *a work of several volumes*

> Parrington, Vernon L. <u>Main</u> <u>Currents</u> <u>in</u> <u>American</u>
>   <u>Thought</u>. 3 vols. New York, 1927–1932.

Volumes, *one of several volumes*

> Perry, Bliss. <u>The</u> <u>American</u> <u>Spirit</u> <u>in</u> <u>Literature</u>, in <u>The</u>
>   <u>Chronicles</u> <u>of</u> <u>America</u> Series, ed. Allen Johnson.
>   48 vols. New Haven, 1918.
>
> > It is seldom necessary to include a specific volume number in the
> > bibliography entry (see below).

Volumes, *component part of one of several volumes*

> Child, Harold. "Jane Austen," in <u>The</u> <u>Cambridge</u> <u>History</u>
>   <u>of</u> <u>English</u> <u>Literature</u>, ed. A. W. Ward and A. R.
>   Waller. London, 1932, XII, 231–244.

or

> Ward, A. W., and A. R. Waller, eds. <u>The</u> <u>Cambridge</u> <u>His-</u>
>   <u>tory</u> <u>of</u> <u>English</u> <u>Literature</u>. 15 vols. London,
>   1932.
>
> > For a discussion of these entries, see p. 119.

Works alphabetically arranged

> Johnson, Allen, ed. <u>The</u> <u>Dictionary</u> <u>of</u> <u>American</u> <u>Biog-</u>
>   <u>raphy</u>. 20 vols. New York, 1927.

or

> Alden, Edmund K., "Alden, John," in <u>The</u> <u>Dictionary</u> <u>of</u>
>   <u>American</u> <u>Biography</u>, ed. Allen Johnson. 20 vols.
>   New York, 1927.
>
> > For a discussion of these entries, see p. 107 and item 2, p. 119.

BIBLIOGRAPHY FORM—PERIODICALS

As you recall, the footnote entry for a periodical article employs the following form:

> [1]Bradford Smith, "Mark Twain and the Mystery of
> Identity," <u>CE</u>, XXIV (March 1963), 426–427.

The bibliography entry for this same reference differs in only three ways:

1. The author's name is flush with the left margin, without a numeral, and with succeeding lines indented approximately five spaces. Enter the surname first, followed by a comma, followed by a given name or initials, followed by a period:

> Smith, Bradford. "Mark Twain and the Mystery of Iden-
>   tity," <u>College</u> <u>English</u>, XXIV (March 1963), 425–
>   430.

2. Spell in full the name of the periodical (see example above).

3. Provide page numbers for the entire article, not for specific pages cited (see example above).

Note below an entry written first for the footnote and then for the bibliography:

> [4]Albert Cohen, "The <u>Fantaisie</u> for Instrumental Ensemble in 17th–Century France––Its Origin and Significance," <u>Mus</u>. <u>Q</u>., XLVIII (March 1960), 62.
>
> Cohen, Albert. "The <u>Fantaisie</u> for Instrumental Ensemble In 17th–Century France––Its Origin and Significance," <u>Music Quarterly</u>, XLVIII (March 1960), 60–104.

Sample Bibliography Entries — Periodicals

Calitri, Charles J. "Love Affair with Words," review of Frank G. Jennings, <u>This Is Reading</u> (New York, 1965), <u>Saturday Review</u>, February 20, 1965, pp. 88–89.

> Note that the above is a weekly magazine, thus no parentheses for dates.

Gibson, James L. "Accounting in the Decision–Making Process," <u>Accounting Review</u> (July 1963), 492–500.

Kilchenmann, Ruth. "Traum und Wirklichkeit in den Werken Friedrich Schnacks," <u>German Quarterly</u>, XXXIV (May 1961), 257–263.

Mothersill, Mary. "Moral Knowledge," <u>Journal of Philosophy</u>, LVI (September 10, 1959), 755–763.

> Since this journal is published fortnightly, yet is paged continuously through each volume, a more specific date is provided.

Phillips, Norma. "The Sacred Fount: The Narrator and the Vampires," <u>PMLA</u>, LXXVI, iv, pt. 1 (September 1961), 407–412.

> Note the additional data to show an issue, paged separately, that appears in two parts. Also, *PMLA* is the name of the journal, not an abbreviation.

Stern, Charlotte. "Sayago and Sayagues in Spanish History and Literature," <u>Hispanic Review</u>, XXIX (July 1961), 217–237.

Thomson, William. "Hindemith's Contribution to Music Theory," <u>Journal of Music Theory</u>, IX, Spring (1965), 52–71.

> The issue number (No. 1) or the name of the issue (Spring) is placed outside the parentheses. Use this form when pagination of the issue is separate and the month of publication is not given.

Ziff, Larzer. "The Other Lost Generation," <u>Saturday Review</u>, February 20, 1965, pp. 15–18.

> Again, note that the above is a weekly publication, thus no parentheses for dates.

BIBLIOGRAPHY FORM—PUBLIC DOCUMENTS

Since the nature of public documents is so varied, the form of the entry cannot be standardized. Therefore, common sense tells you to provide sufficient information so that the reader can easily locate the reference. Note the following:

U.S. Bureau of the Budget. <u>Special Analysis</u>: <u>Budget of the United States</u>. Fiscal year 1967. Washington, D.C., 1966.

Higher Education Act of 1965. 79 Stat. (1965).

> Compare *Swain v. Alabama* below. Court cases and legislative acts follow a form stipulated by law publications. The act or case is listed first, followed by the volume number, abbreviated title, the date of the work in which the act or case is found. Also, notice that the volume number is in arabic numerals, that the date is placed within parentheses, and that a court case is italicized but an act is not.

Kansas. <u>Session Laws 1963</u>.

> Normally, the date is placed in parentheses, but in this case the date is a part of the title.

U.S. Congress. <u>Senate Joint Resolution 1</u>. 89th Cong., 1st sess., 1965.

U.S. <u>Congressional Record</u>. Vol. CX.

U.S. <u>Constitution</u>. Art. 2, sec. 1.

U.S. Department of State. <u>Foreign Relations of the United States</u>: <u>Diplomatic Papers, 1943</u>. Washington, D.C., 1944.

U.S. Department of State. <u>United States Treaties and Other International Agreements</u>. XV, Part 1, 1964.

U.S. House of Representatives. Committee on Interstate and Foreign Commerce. <u>Federal Cigarette Labeling and Advertising Act</u>. 89th Cong., 1st sess., 1965. H. Rept. 449 to accompany H. R. 3014.

U.S. President. <u>Public Papers of the Presidents of the United States</u>. Washington, D.C., 1964.

U.S. Senate. Committee on Foreign Relations. <u>Hearings on S. 2793, Supplemental Foreign Assistance Fiscal Year 1966--Vietnam</u>. 89th Cong., 2nd sess., 1966.

U.S. Senate. <u>The Constitution of the United States of America</u>: <u>Analysis and Interpretation</u>. Senate Document 170, 82nd Cong., 2nd sess., 1952.

U.S. <u>Statutes at Large</u>. LXXVIII, 990.

U.S. <u>Statutes at Large</u>. LXXII, Part 1, 455.

BIBLIOGRAPHY FORM—OTHER SOURCES
Bulletin

> French, Earl. "Personal Problems in Industrial Research
> and Development." Ithaca, N.Y., 1963. (Bulletin
> of the New York State School of Industrial and
> Labor Relations, No. 51.)

Dissertation, *published*

> Katz, Joseph. <u>Plotinus' Search for the Good</u>.
> Dissertation, New York, 1950.

Dissertation, *unpublished*

> Hitchcock, James Francis. "Popular Religion in
> Elizabethan England." Unpublished dissertation.
> Princeton University, 1965.

Interview

> Interview with R. Earl Farnsworth, Principal, Northside
> High School, Fort Smith, Ark., January 4, 1966.

> Interview with Hans Conreid, stage and television
> personality, Emporia, Kansas, February 21,
> 1966.

Leaflet

> See "Pamphlet," p. 129.

Lecture

> Jones, Charles. "Thomas Jefferson." Emporia, Kansas,
> 1965. (Lecture presented at Kansas State Teachers
> College.)

Letter, *personal*

> Information in a letter to the author from William Inge,
> playwright, February 4, 1966.

> Information in a letter to the author from Professor
> David S. Berkeley of Oklahoma State University,
> March 6, 1966.

Mimeographed material

> Smith, Jane. "Terms for the Study of Fiction." Oklahoma
> City, 1965. (Mimeographed.)

Monograph

> NEA Research Division. <u>Kindergarten Practices, 1961</u>.
> Washington, D.C., 1962. (Monograph 1962-M2.)

Newspaper

> Editorial, <u>The Kansas City Star</u>, March 19, 1966, p. 52.

> Speaight, Robert. "No Final Pessimism in Tragedy of
> Lear," <u>The Kansas City Times</u>, May 2, 1965, p. 1G.

Pamphlet

> Ray, William S. "Common Sense in Behavioral Research."
> Greensboro, N.C., 1963. (Pamphlet of the Institute
> for Child and Family Development.)

Public address

> Sarnoff, David. "Television: A Channel for Freedom."
> Detroit, 1961. (Address presented at the
> University of Detroit Academic Convocation.)

Recording

> "Chaucer: The Nun's Priest's Tale." Narrated in Middle
> English by Robert Ross. Caedmon Recording, No.
> E8C40.

> "I Can Hear It Now: Winston Churchill," ed. Edward R.
> Murrow and Fred W. Friendly. Narrator, Edward R.
> Murrow. Columbia Masterworks Recording, No.
> E9C10.

Report

> Scheer, Robert. "How the United States Got Involved in
> Vietnam." Santa Barbara, Calif., 1965. (Re-
> port to the Center for the Study of Democratic
> Institutions.)

> Mellon Institute Research. Fifty–First Annual Report.
> Pittsburgh, 1964.

Source books

> Wasserstrom, William. "Cooper, Freud and the Origins of
> Culture," The American Imago, XVII, Winter (1960),
> 423–437. Reprinted in Leatherstocking and the
> Critics, ed. Warren S. Walker. Chicago, 1965.

or

> Walker, Warren S., ed. Leatherstocking and the Critics.
> Chicago, 1965.
>> Use the form of the first entry if your instructor expects a bibliography
>> entry for each article from which you cite; otherwise, the form of the
>> alternate entry is sufficient.

> Poe, Edgar Allan. "The Poetic Principle," The Complete
> Works of Edgar Allan Poe, ed. James A. Harrison.
> New York, 1902. Reprinted in Tolstoy and the
> Critics: Literature and Aesthetics, ed. Holley
> G. Duffield and Manuel Bilsky. Chicago, 1965.

Television or radio program

> "Town Meeting of the World," C.B.S. telecast, March 1,
> 1966: "Nuclear Proliferation." Narrator, Eric
> Severeid.

Thesis, *published*

See "Dissertation, published," p. 128.

Thesis, *unpublished*

Simpson, Herman H.   "A Study of Shakespeare's Departures
     from Plutarch in the Characterization of Cleopatra
     in <u>Antony</u> <u>and</u> <u>Cleopatra</u>."   Unpublished thesis.
     Oklahoma State University, 1961.

Unpublished paper

Elkins, William R.   "The Dream World and the Dream
     Vision: Meaning and Structure in Poe's Art."
     (Unpublished paper.)

DOCUMENTATION
OF SCIENCE PAPERS

You may discover that your science instructor requires a system of documentation quite different from that described in the preceding two chapters. Accordingly, when you write a research paper in the fields of biological science, physical science, mathematics, or psychology, you should consult this chapter, which is intended to supply a brief but adequate description of science-paper documentation. However, you should realize at the start that modifications of style exist from field to field, and agreement does not always exist within a given discipline. Nevertheless, after consultation with your instructor, you should find one of the two systems outlined below satisfactory for your needs.

As a general rule, science papers, excluding those dealing with physics (see p. 137), require no footnotes except content footnotes (see p. 115). Instead, you insert, within your text, reference numbers (1) or reference dates (1967). Then, at the end of your paper, you list, numerically or alphabetically, only those references actually mentioned in your text. You may label the list as "List of References" or "Literature Cited." The title "Bibliography" seldom appears in science papers.

In addition, you should note other characteristics of the reference entries. First, you will usually capitalize only the first word of titles of books and articles (for example, "The biology of the algae"). But some fields (for example, chemistry and physics) omit completely the title of a periodical article. Second, you will usually abbreviate and seldom underline the name of the periodical (for example, "Amer. J. Bot."; see pp. 149-151, 153-154 for listings of science journals and their standard abbreviations). But you should note that the field of psychology, since 1963, spells in full the names of periodicals. Third, you will usually write the volume numbers in arabic numbers, although placement and form will vary (for example, "vol. 70" or "70").

Name and Year System

When employing the name and year system, you should place within your text, in parentheses or brackets, the year of publication of the authority's book or journal article. Furthermore:

1. Place the entry immediately after the authority's name:

```
    Smith (1965) ascribes no species-specific

    behavior to man.  However, Adams (1967)

    presents data that tend to be contradictory.
```

2. If your sentence construction does not require the use of the authority's name, insert both the name and date in parentheses:

```
    Hopkins (1966) found some supporting evidence

    for a portion of the Marr data (Marr and Brown,

    1957) through point bi-serial correlation

    techniques.
```

3. For two authors, employ both names: "(Torgerson and Andrews, 1967)." For three authors, name them all in the first entry, as "(Torgerson, Andrews, and Dunlap, 1967)," but thereafter use "(Torgerson et al., 1967)." For four or more authors, employ "Fredericks et al. (1966)" in the first instance.

4. Use small letters (a, b, c) to identify two or more works published in the same year by the same author, for example, "Thompson (1966a)" and "Thompson (1966b)."

5. If necessary, specify additional information; for example, "Thompson (1967, III)," "(Wallace, 1948, 1967)," and "White and Thurston (1967, 211–214)":

```
    Horton (1966; cf. Thomas, 1962, p. 89) suggests

    an intercorrelation of these testing devices.

    But after multiple-group analysis, Welston (1967,

    p. 211) reached an opposite conclusion.
```

6. Alphabetize the "List of References" at the end of your paper. List chronologically two or more works by the same author (for example, Fitzgerald's publication of 1964 would precede his 1967 publication).

A sample "List of References"[1] follows:

```
                      List of References


Esau, K. 1965. Plant anatomy. John Wiley and
     Sons, New York. 735 p.

Jensen, W. A. 1962. Botanical histochemistry.
     W. H. Freeman, New York. 408 p.

Olive, L. S. 1962. The genus Protostelium.
     Amer. J. Bot. 49: 297-303.

-------. 1964a. Spore discharge mechanism in
     basidiomycetes. Science 146: 542-543.

-------. 1964b. A new member of the Mycetozoa.
     Mycologia 61: 885-896.

Round, F. E. 1965. The biology of the algae.
     St. Martin's Press, New York. 269 p.
```

Fig. 40: Sample List of References

The Number System

After completing your "List of References," you should assign a number to each entry. Then, to designate your source of information, you should employ the appropriate number within your text. Furthermore:

1. Place the entry, enclosed within parentheses (or brackets), immediately after the authority's name:

[1]The form of these botany entries conforms to the *American Journal of Botany, The Botanical Review,* and the American Institute of Biological Sciences, *Style Manual for Biological Journals* (Washington, D.C., 1960).

```
        In particular the recent paper by Hershel,

    Hobbs, and Thomason (1) raises many interesting

    questions related to photosynthesis, some of

    which were answered by Skelton (2), (3).
```

2. If the sentence construction does not require the use of the authority's name, employ one of the following three methods:

a. Insert both name and number within parentheses:

```
    Additional observations include alterations in

    carbohydrate metabolism (Evans, 3), changes in

    ascorbic acid incorporation into the cell (Dodd

    and Williams, 11) and adjoining membranes

    (Holt and Zimmer, 7).
```

b. Insert both name and number within parentheses and enclose the number within brackets (few journals use this method):

```
    The subject of the cytochrome oxidase system

    in cell metabolism has received a great deal

    of attention (Singleton [4]).
```

c. Insert the number only, enclosing it within parentheses (or brackets):

```
    It is known (1) that the DNA concentration of

    a nucleus doubles during interphase.
```

3. If necessary, add specific data to the entry (for example, "[3, Proposition 8]" or "[6, p. 76]"):

The results of the respiration experiment

published by Jones (3, p. 412) had been

predicted earlier by Smith (5).

Arrange your references in alphabetical order and number them consecutively through the list of references (in which case the numbers will not appear in consecutive order in your text), *or* forego an alphabetical arrangement and number the references consecutively as they appear in the text, interrupting that order in your text when entering an earlier reference.

A numbered, alphabetized list follows:[1]

Literature Cited

1. Griffeth, T., K. P. Hellman, and R. V. Byerrum. 1960. Studies on the biogenesis of the ring systems of nicotine. J. Biol. Chem. 235: 800–804.

2. Hodson, P. H., and J. W. Foster. 1966. Dipicolinic acid synthesis in Penicillium citreoviride. J. Bacteriol. 91: 562–569.

3. Kanie, J., S. Fujimoto, and J. W. Foster. 1966. Chemical degradation of dipicolinic acid–C^{14} and its application in biosynthesis by Penicillium citreoviride. J. Bacteriol. 91: 570–577.

4. Krebs, H. A., and S. M. Lowenstein. 1960. The tricarboxylic acid cycle, p. 129–203. In D. M. Greenberg [ed.], Metabolic pathways, vol. 1. Academic Press, Inc., New York.

5. Meister, A. 1965. Biochemistry of the amino acids, 2nd ed., vol. 2. Academic Press, Inc., New York.

6. Smith, I. [ed.] 1960. Chromatographic and electrophoretic techniques, vol. 1. Chromatography. Interscience Publishers, Inc., New York.

Fig. 41: Literature Cited

[1]The form of these biology entries conforms to the American Institute of Biological Sciences, *Style Manual for Biological Journals* (Washington, D.C., 1960). See also "List of References," p. 133.

SAMPLE FORMS OF ENTRIES FOR THE VARIOUS SCIENCE DISCIPLINES

Biology

See above, "Literature Cited," p. 135.

Botany

See above, "List of References," p. 133.

Chemistry[1]

(1) G. C. Pimentel, "The Hydrogen Bond," W. H. Freeman Co., San Francisco, Calif., 1960.

(2) J. D. Corbett in "Fused Salts," B. R. Sundheim, Ed., McGraw-Hill Book Co., Inc., New York, 1964, p. 341.

(3) W. H. Baddley, Ph.D. Dissertation, Northwestern University, Evanston, Ill., 1964.

(4) L. Barton, S. K. Wason, and R. F. Porter, J. Phys. Chem., 69, 3160 (1965).

(5) G. C. Berry and T. G. Fox, J. Am. Chem. Soc., 86, 3540 (1964).

(6) J. R. Morton, Chem. Rev., 64, 452 (1964).

Geology[2]

Donath, F. A., 1963, Strength variation and deformational behavior in anisotropic rock, p. 281-297 in Judd, Wm. R., Editor, State of stress in the earth's crust: New York, American Elsevier Publishing Co., Inc., 732 p.

Friedlander, G., Kennedy, J. W., and Miller, J. M., 1964, Nuclear and radiochemistry: New York, John Wiley and Sons, 585 p.

Harker, Alfred, 1965, The natural history of igneous rocks: New York, Hafner, 384 p.

Heard, H. C., Turner, F. J., and Weiss, L. E., 1965, Studies of heterogeneous strain in experimentally deformed calcite, marble, and phyllite: Univ. Calif. Pub. Geol. Sci., v. 46, p. 81-152.

Hill, M. L., and Troxel, B. W., 1966, Tectonics of Death Valley region, California: Geol. Soc. America Bull., v. 77, p. 435-438.

O'Keefe, J. A., and Adams, E. W., 1965, Tektite structure and lunar ash flows: Jour. Geophys. Research, v. 70, p. 3819-3829.

---

[1]The form of these chemistry entries conforms to the *Journal of American Chemical Society* and the *Journal of Physical Chemistry*.

[2]The form of these geology entries conforms to *The Journal of Geology, Geological Society of America Bulletin*, and *American Journal of Science*.

Mathematics[1]

1. R. Artzy, Linear geometry, Addison-Wesley, Reading, Mass., 1965.

2. W. M. Frank, A bound on determinants, Proc. Amer. Math. Soc. 16 (1965), 360–363.

3. I. M. Isaacs and D. S. Passman, Groups with representations of bounded degree, Canad. J. Math. 16 (1964), 299–309.

4. ------, Characterization of groups in terms of the degrees of their characters, Pacific J. Math. 15 (1965), 877–903.

5. C. E. Rickart, General theory of Banach algebras, Van Nostrand, Princeton, N.J., 1960.

6. O. Solbrig, Evolution and systematics, The Macmillan Co., New York, 1966.

Physics[2]

[1]F. Riesz and Bela Nagy, Functional Analysis (Frederick Ungar Publishing Company, New York, 1955), Secs. 121 and 123.

[2]S. Bergia and L. Brown, In Proceedings of the International Conference on Nucleon Structure, edited by R. Hofstadter and L. I. Schiff (Stanford University Press, Stanford, California, 1963), p. 320.

[3]Oswald H. Blackwood, William C. Kelly, Raymond M. Bell, General Physics (John Wiley and Sons, Inc., New York, 1963), p. 510.

[4]T. D. Lee, Phys. Rev. 139, B1415 (1965).

[5]K. Gottfried and J. D. Jackson, Nuovo Cimento 22, 309 (1964).

[6]E. T. Jaynes, Am. J. Phys. 33, 391 (1965).

Psychology[3]

Attneave, F. Dimensions of similarity. American Journal of Psychology, 1950, 63, 516–556.

Gaito, John. (Ed.) Macromolecules and behavior. New York: Appleton-Century-Crofts, 1966.

Harvey, O. J., Hunt, D. E., & Schroder, H. M. Conceptual systems of personality organization. New York: Wiley, 1961.

[1]The form of these math entries conforms to the *Proceedings of the American Mathematical Society.*

[2]Rather than placing these physics notes in a "List of References" at the end of your paper, you should place them as footnotes at the bottom of the page on which the citation appears. The form of these entries conforms to *The Physical Review* and *American Journal of Physics.*

[3]The form of these psychology entries conforms generally to The American Psychological Association, *Publication Manual*, 1957 Revision (Washington, D.C., 1957).

Horman, Louis M.   Information encoding and decision time
    as variables in human choice behavior. <u>Journal
    of</u> Experimental Psychology, 1966, <u>71</u> (5), 718–724.

Keniston, Kenneth. <u>The uncommitted</u>: <u>alienated youth in
    American society</u>. New York: Harcourt, Brace &
    World, 1966.

Vannoy, J. S.   Generality of cognitive complexity–
    simplicity as a personality construct. <u>Journal
    of</u> Personality <u>and</u> Social Psychology, 1965, <u>2</u>,
    385–396.

Zoology

See biology, p. 136, and botany, p. 136.

A GLOSSARY OF ADDITIONAL RESEARCH TERMS

Accents Place where necessary in ink, by hand (for example, *cliché, précis*). To determine the correct accents for foreign words, consult an appropriate foreign language dictionary.

Acknowledgments Place necessary acknowledgments or explanations in a footnote to your first sentence:

> [1]I wish here to express my thanks to Mrs. Horace
> A. Humphrey for permission to examine the manuscripts of
> her late husband.

Usually, there is no need for a preface in a research paper.

Ampersand Avoid using the ampersand symbol "&." Instead, spell out the "and" in the name of a company or organization, unless custom demands it, e.g., "A&P."

Annotated Bibliography Write descriptive notes for each entry.

Appendix Place additional material in an appendix at the end of your paper. It is a logical location for numerous tables and illustrations or other accumulated data.

Apostrophe Add an apostrophe and *s* to form the possessive of one-syllable proper names that end in *s* or another sibilant (for example, "Keats's poem," "Rice's story," "Bates's *The Kinds of Man*"). In words of more than one syllable ending in a sibilant, add the apostrophe only (for example, "Rawlings' novel," "Evans' essay," "Daiches' criticism"), except for names ending in a sibilant and a final *e* (for example, "Lovelace's enduring appeal").

Arabic Numerals Generally, spell out numbers of less than three digits (for example, "four," "sixteen," "345"), but use numerals for *all* numbers in a paragraph that contains both types. Always spell out numbers that begin sentences. Use the small "l," not a capital "I," when typing the numeral "one." Samples of correct usage:

> A.D. 200 <u>but</u> 200 B.C.
> Art. 3

```
│:0│   5
eighteenth of November or November 18, 1966
Fig. 6
in 1966-67 or from 1966 to 1967, but not from 1966-67
11. 32-34
March 5, 1935 or 5 March 1935, but not both styles
1960's but sixties
one-fifth but 153½ (for three or more digits)
pp. 121-122
pp. 1151-53 but pp. 1193-1215
Sec. 3
6 per cent
six o'clock or 6:00 p.m.
6.213
twentieth century
```

Asterisks Use arabic numerals for footnote numbers and asterisks only for footnoting illustrations or tables (see Fig. 47, p. 147)

Bible Use parenthetical documentation for biblical references in your text—that is, place the entry within parentheses immediately after the quotation, for example, "(II Kings.xviii. 13)." Do not underline titles of books of the Bible. Abbreviations of most books of the Bible follow (but do not abbreviate one-syllable titles, for example, "Mark" or "Acts"):

I and II Chron.	I and II Chronicles	Lev.	Leviticus
Col.	Colossians	Mal.	Malachi
I and II Cor.	I and II Corinthians	Matt.	Matthew
Dan.	Daniel	Mic.	Micah
Deut.	Deuteronomy	Nah.	Nahum
Eccles.	Ecclesiastes	Neh.	Nehemiah
Eph.	Ephesians	Num.	Numbers
Exod.	Exodus	Obad.	Obadiah
Ezek.	Ezekiel	I and II Pet.	I and II Peter
Gal.	Galatians	Phil.	Philippians
Gen.	Genesis	Prov.	Proverbs
Hab.	Habakkuk	Ps.(Pss.)	Psalm(s)
Hag.	Haggai	Rev.	Revelation
Heb.	Hebrews	Rom.	Romans
Hos.	Hosea	I and II Sam.	I and II Samuel
Isa.	Isaiah	Song of Sol.	Song of Solomon
Jas.	James	I and II Thess.	I and II Thessalonians
Jer.	Jeremiah	I and II Tim.	I and II Timothy
Josh.	Joshua	Zech.	Zechariah
Judg.	Judges	Zeph.	Zephaniah
Lam.	Lamentations		

Capitalization Titles of books: capitalize the first word and all principal words, but not articles, prepositions, and conjunctions (for example, *The Last of the Mohicans*).

Titles of magazines and newspapers: as above, except do not treat an initial definite article as part of the title except when the title is entered separately as a source:

```
"He was referring to the Kansas City Star and. . . ."

10Editorial, The Kansas City Star, March 18, 1966,
     p. 43D.
```

Titles of parts of a specific work: capitalize as for books (for example, "Thompson's Appendix II," "Jones's Preface," "Writing the Final Draft").

Titles of French, Italian, and Spanish works: capitalize the first word, the proper nouns, but not adjectives derived from proper nouns.

Titles of German works: capitalize the first word, all nouns, and all adjectives derived from names of persons.

Abbreviations: capitalize a noun followed by a numeral indicating place in a sequence (for example, "Act II," "Ch. iv," "No. 14," "Vol. III"). Do not capitalize "l.," "n.," "p.," or "sig."

Dash Form the dash with two typed hyphens with no space before or after:

```
The professions that require intelligent, analytic minds
--medicine, law, teaching--attract too few young people.
```

See also p. 147 for sample of the dash in documentation.

Dates Follow these examples:

```
14 March or March 14, not the fourteenth of March
14 March 1967 or March 14, 1967, but consistently use
   one style
March 1967 or March, 1967, but consistently use one
   style
1960's or sixties
in 1966-67 or from 1966 to 1967, but not from 1966-67
150 B.C. but A.D. 150
fourteenth century but 14th century in footnotes
```

Definitions For definitions within your text, use single quotation marks without intervening punctuation (for example, "*et alii* 'and others'").

Enumeration of Items Incorporate short items into the text, as follows:

```
College instructors are usually divided into four ranks:
(1) instructors, (2) assistant professors, (3) associate
professors, and (4) full professors.
```

Present longer items in a tabular form, as follows:

```
College instructors are usually divided into four ranks:

   1. Instructors, at the bottom of the scale, are usually
      beginning teachers with little or no experience.
   2. Assistant professors. . . .
```

Etc. *Et cetera* 'and so forth': avoid using in the text by listing at least four items, as follows:

```
Images of color occur frequently in Crane's writing,
especially blue, gold, red, and grey.
```

Foreign Languages Underline foreign words used in an English text:

```
Like his friend Olaf, he is aut Caesar, aut nihil,
either overpowering perfection or ruin and destruction.
```

Do not underline quotations:

> Obviously, he uses it to exploit, in the words of Jean
> Laumon, "une admirable mine de thèmes poétiques."

Do not underline titles of magazine articles:

> [3]Von Thomas O. Brandt, "Brecht und die Bibel,"
> PMLA, LXXIX (March 1964), 171.

Do not underline places, institutions, proper names, or titles that precede proper names:

> Of course, Racine became extremely fond of Mlle Champ-
> meslé, who interpreted his works at the Hôtel de Bour-
> gogne.

Illustrations and Tables A table is a systematic arrangement of statistical materials, usually in columns. An illustration is any item that is not a table: blueprint, chart, diagram, drawing, graph, photograph, photostat, map, and so on. Note the following samples:

Fig. 42: Illustration

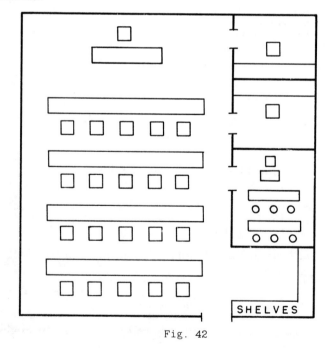

Fig. 42

Audio Laboratory With Private Listening Rooms and a
Small Group Room

Fig. 43: Table

TABLE I

RESPONSE BY CLASS ON VIETNAM POLICY

	Freshmen	Sophomores	Juniors	Seniors
1. Holding action	2	7	19	0
2. Withdrawal	150	137	111	78
3. Escalation	296	301	229	187

When presenting an illustration or table in your research paper, conform to the following stipulations:

1. Present only one kind of information in each illustration, making it as simple and as brief as possible; frills and fancy art work may distract rather than attract the reader.

2. Place small illustrations within your text. Large illustrations should go on a separate page. If you have numerous illustrations or long, complex tables, these should be placed in an appendix at the end of your paper.

3. Place the illustration as near to your textual discussion as possible, although the illustration should not precede your first mention of it.

4. Make certain that your textual discussion adequately explains the significance of the illustration. Follow two rules: (1) write the illustration so that your reader can understand it without reference to your discussion; and (2) write your discussion of the illustration so that your reader may understand your observations without reference to the illustration. But avoid giving too many numbers and figures in your text.

5. In your textual discussion refer to illustrations by number (for example, "Figure 5" or "Table IV, p. 16"), not by a vague reference (for example, "the table above," "the following illustration," or "the chart below").

6. Number illustrations consecutively throughout the paper with arabic numbers, preceded by "Fig." or "Figure" (for example, "Figure 4"), placed one double space above the caption and centered on the page *below* the illustration.

7. Number tables consecutively throughout the paper with capital roman numerals, preceded by "Table" (for example, "Table II"), placed one double space above the caption and centered on the page *above* the table.

8. Always insert a caption that explains the illustration, placed *above* the table and *below* the illustration, centered, in full capital letters

or in capitals and lower case, but do not mix forms in the same paper. An alternative is to place the caption on the same line with the number (see Figure 44 below).

9. Insert a caption or number for each column of a table, centered above the column or, if necessary, inserted diagonally or vertically above it.

10. When inserting an explanatory or reference footnote, place it below both a table and an illustration; then use an asterisk as the identifying superscript, not an arabic numeral (for example, see Figs. 46 and 47, p. 146).

Note the following samples of charts and illustrations such as you might use in a research paper:

Fig. 44: Illustration

Fig. 44: Mean Number of Matches by Subjects With and Without Standards (By Trial). From Edwin A. Locke and Judith F. Bryan, "Cognitive Aspects of Psychomotor Performance," _Journal_ _of_ _Applied_ _Psychology_, L (August 1966), 289.

Fig. 45: Illustration

SUPRASEGMENTAL

STRESS ╱   ⋀   ╲   ⋃

(primary)   (secondary)   (tertiary)   (weak)

PITCH

  1   2   3   4 (relatively rare)

(low)   (average)   (high)   (exceptionally high)

<u>Juncture</u>

   open

�osed at minor break, usually between words

   terminal

     or ⟶ "level"

     at greater break within sentence, also in

       apposition;

           level pitch

     or ⟋ "rising"

     in "yes–no" questions, series;

         pitch–rise before the pause

     or ⟍ "falling"

     at end of most sentences;

         pitch–drop, voice fades off

Fig. 45: Phonemes of English. Generally, this figure follows the Trager–Smith system, used widely in American linguistics. From Anna H. Live, "Pattern in Language," <u>The</u> <u>Journal</u> <u>of</u> <u>General</u> <u>Education</u>, XVIII (July 1966), 94.

Fig. 46: Table

TABLE II*

Mean Scores of Six Values Held by College

Students According to Sex

All Students		Men		Women	
Pol.	40.61	Pol.	43.22	Aesth.	43.86
Rel.	40.51	Theor.	43.09	Rel.	43.13
Aesth.	40.29	Econ.	42.05	Soc.	41.62
Theor.	39.80	Rel.	37.88	Pol.	38.00
Econ.	39.45	Soc.	37.05	Econ.	36.85
Soc.	39.34	Aesth.	36.72	Theor.	36.50

*From Carmen J. Finley, Jack M. Thompson, and Albert Cognata, "Stability of the California Short Form Test of Mental Maturity: Grades 3, 5, and 7," California Journal of Educational Research, XVII (September 1966), 165.

Fig. 47: Table

TABLE III. Inhibitory effects of sugars on the growth of Clostridium histolyticum (11 strains) on nutrient agar*

Sugar added (2%)	Aerobic incubation (hr)		Anaerobic incubation (hr)	
	24	48	24	48
None	11**	11	11	11
Glucose	0	0	11	11
Maltose	0	0	11	11
Lactose	1	1	11	11
Sucrose	3	6	11	11
Arabinose	0	0	0	0
Inositol	0	0	11	11
Xylose	0	0	0	0
Sorbitol	2	7	11	11
Mannitol	9	10	11	11
Rhamnose	0	0	11	11

*From Shoki Nishida and Masaaki Imaizumi. 1966. Toxigenicity of Clostridium histolyticum. J. Bacteriol. 91:481.
**No. of strains which gave rise to colonies in the presence of the sugar.

Parenthetical Documentation Handle references within sentences in one of the following ways:

According to William C. DeVane, A Browning Handbook (New York, 1955), p. 37, Browning's liberalism follows the doctrine of Victorian laissez-faire.

or

```
According to William C. DeVane--A Browning Handbook (New
York, 1955), p. 37--Browning's liberalism follows the
doctrine of Victorian laissez-faire.
```

If these forms prove awkward, recast the sentence so that the documentation comes at the end:

```
Browning's laissez-faire liberalism is stressed by
William C. DeVane, A Browning Handbook (New York, 1955),
p. 37.
```

Punctuation of Quotations In every instance, place commas and periods *inside* the quotation marks but semicolons and colons *outside* the quotation marks. Place the question mark and the exclamation mark inside the quotation marks if the mark is part of the quoted material; otherwise, place it outside the quotation marks:

```
The philosopher asks, "How should we order our lives?"
```

```
How should we order our lives when we face "hostility
from every quarter"?
```

Roman Numerals Use capital or small roman numerals as shown below:

```
Act II          Bk. x
Vol. III        Chap. xi
Part IV         scene xii
Div. V          canto xiii
Plate VI        pp. xiv-xvii
Table VII
```

A list of roman numerals:

	UNITS	TENS	HUNDREDS
1	i	x	c
2	ii	xx	cc
3	iii	xxx	ccc
4	iv	xl	cd
5	v	l	d
6	vi	lx	dc
7	vii	lxx	dcc
8	viii	lxxx	dcccc
9	ix	xc	cm

Shakespearean Plays For use in parenthetical documentation, *Shakespeare Quarterly* suggests the following abbreviations of titles of Shakespearean plays: *All's W., Antony, A.Y.L., Errors, Cor., Cym., Ham., 1 H.IV, Caesar, John, Lear, L.L.L., Macb., Meas., Merch., Wives, Dream, Much, Oth., Per., R.II, R.III, Romeo, Shrew, Temp., Tim., Tit., Troi., T.G.V.*; also *Venus, Lucr., Sonn., Lov.Com., Pass.Pil., Phoenix.*

Slang Enclose in double quotation marks any words to which you direct attention.

Underlining Underline the following: books, bulletins, pamphlets, periodicals, plays, motion pictures, newspapers, operas, ships, symphonies, and yearbooks. If separately published, underline the following: essays, lectures, poems, proceedings, reports, sermons, and stories.

Word Division When necessary, divide a word with a hyphen so that the break comes between two syllables, but avoid one-letter and two-letter division (for example, "o-ver" or "separate-ly"). When in doubt about the proper division of a word, always consult a dictionary.

LIST OF GENERAL REFERENCE BOOKS AND JOURNALS

Applied Sciences

GENERAL

Books

Annual Review of Nuclear Science. Stanford, Calif., 1952–date.

Applied Science and Technology Index. New York, 1913–date.

Ballentyne, D. W. G., and L. E. Q. Walker. A Dictionary of Named Effects and Laws in Chemistry, Physics, and Mathematics. 2nd ed., rev. New York, 1961.

Besserer, C. W., and H. C. Besserer. Guide to the Space Age. Englewood Cliffs, N. J., 1959.

Hawkins, R. R., ed. Scientific, Medical, and Technical Books Published in the United States of America. 2nd ed. Washington, D. C., 1958.

Hodgman, Charles D., ed. Handbook of Chemistry and Physics. 31st ed. Cleveland, 1949.

McGraw-Hill Encyclopedia of Science and Technology. Rev. ed. 15 vols. New York, 1966.

Mellon, M. G. Chemical Publications: Their Use and Nature. 4th ed. New York, 1965.

Michels, Walter C., et al. The International Dictionary of Physics and Electronics. Princeton, N. J., 1956.

Pearl, Richard M. Guide to Geologic Literature. New York, 1951.

Tannehill, Ivan R. Weather Around the World. Princeton, N. J., 1943.

Technical Book Review Index. New York, 1935–date.

Tower, Merrell E. Student Guide for Aeronautics. 2nd ed. Los Angeles, 1952.

Tweney, C. F., and L. E. C. Hughes, eds. Chambers's Technical Dictionary. 3rd ed., rev. New York, 1958.

United Nations Atomic Energy Commission Group. An International Bibliography on Atomic Energy. 2 vols. Lake Success, 1949–1951.

U.S. Library of Congress. Science and Technology Division. Air Force Scientific Research Bibliography, 1950–1956, ed. G. Vernon Hooker et al. Washington, 1961–. (In progress.)

CHEMICAL ENGINEERING

Books

Cremer, Herbert W., and Trefor Davis. Chemical Engineering Practice. London, 1956–1960.

Perry, John H., ed. Chemical Engineer's Handbook. 2nd ed. New York, 1941.

Journals

Chemical and Engineering News (Chem. & Eng. N.)

Chemical Engineering (Chem. Eng.)

Industrial and Engineering Chemistry (Ind. & Eng. Chem.)

Industrial and Engineering Chemistry Fundamentals (Ind. & Eng. Chem. Fund.)

CHEMISTRY

Books

American Chemical Society. Chemical Abstracts. Columbus, Ohio, 1907–date.

Clark, George L., et al. The Encyclopedia of Chemistry. New York, 1957. Supplement, 1958.

Crane, Evan J., et al. A Guide to the Literature of Chemistry. 2nd ed. New York, 1957.

Kirk, Raymond E., and D. F. Othmer. Encyclopedia of Chemical Technology. 2nd ed. New York, 1963–. (In progress.)

Lange, Norbert A. Handbook of Chemistry. Sandusky, Ohio, 1934–date.

Rose, Arthur, and Elizabeth Rose. *The Condensed Chemical Dictionary.* 6th ed. New York, 1961.

Soule, Byron A. *Library Guide for the Chemist.* New York, 1938.

Thorpe, Jocelyn F., and M. A. Whiteley. *Thorpe's Dictionary of Applied Chemistry.* 4th ed. 12 vols. New York, 1937 – 1956.

Journals

Chemical Abstracts (Chem. Abstr.)
Chemical Abstracts Collective Index
Chemical Abstracts Decennial Indexes
Chemical News (Chem. N.)
Chemical Reviews (Chem. Rev.)
Chemical Society, Proceedings (Chem. Soc. Proc.)
Chemical Titles
Chemistry (Chem.)
Journal of American Chemical Society (J. Am. Chem. Soc.)
Journal of Chemical Documentation (J. Chem. Document.)
Journal of Chemical Education (J. Chem. Educ.)

ELECTRONICS

Books

Carr, Clifford C. *American Electrician's Handbook.* 8th ed. New York, 1961.

Henney, Keith. *The Radio Engineering Handbook.* 4th ed. New York, 1950.

Knowlton, Archer E., ed. *Standard Handbook for Electrical Engineers.* New York, 1957.

Special Libraries Association. Electrical Engineering Committee. *A Bibliography of Electrical Literature, Current Sources, and Reference Books.* Providence, R. I., 1928.

Journals

Electronic Age (Elec. Age)
Electronics
Electronics World (Elec. World)

ENGINEERING

Books

Dapples, Edward C. *Basic Geology for Science and Engineering.* New York, 1959.

Johnson, Irma. *Selected Books and Journals in Science and Engineering.* 2nd ed. Cambridge, Mass., 1958.

Jones, Franklin D. *Engineering Encyclopedia.* 2nd ed. 2 vols. New York, 1943.

Kent, William. *Mechanical Engineers' Handbook.* 12th ed. 2 vols. New York, 1960 – 1961.

O'Rourke, Charles E., ed. *General Engineering Handbook.* 2nd ed. New York, 1940.

Trautwine, John C. *The Civil Engineer's Pocket-Book.* Philadelphia, 1922.

Journals

General Electric Review (Gen. Elec. Rev.)
Journal of Engineering Education (J. Eng. Educ.)

MATHEMATICS

Books

Baer, Reinhold. *Linear Algebra and Projective Geometry.* New York, 1952.

Begle, Edward G. *Introductory Calculus, With Analytic Geometry.* New York, 1954.

Coxeter, H. S. M. *Non-Euclidean Geometry.* 3rd ed. Toronto, 1957.

Eves, Howard, and C. V. Newsom. *Introduction to the Foundations and Fundamental Concepts of Mathematics.* New York, 1958.

Feferman, Solomon. *The Number Systems: Foundations of Algebra and Analysis.* Reading, Mass., 1964.

Feller, William. *An Introduction to Probability Theory and Its Applications.* 2nd ed. New York, 1957.

Fletcher, Alan, et al. *An Index of Mathematical Tables.* 2nd ed. Reading, Mass., 1962.

Guggenheim, Heinrich W. *Differential Geometry.* New York, 1963.

Halmos, Paul R. *Naive Set Theory.* Princeton, N. J., 1960.

Hurewicz, Witold, and H. Wallman. *Dimension Theory.* Rev. ed. Princeton, N. J., 1948.

James, Glenn, and Robert C. James, eds. *Mathematics Dictionary.* 2nd ed. Princeton, N. J., 1959.

Kelly, John L. *General Topology.* Princeton, N. J., 1955.

Landau, Edmund G. H. *Elementary Number Theory,* tr. Jacob E. Goodman. New York, 1958.

Lefschetz, Solomon. *Introduction to Topology.* Princeton, N. J., 1949.

Mood, Alexander M., and F. A. Graybill. *Introduction to the Theory of Statistics.* 2nd ed. New York, 1963.

National Council of Teachers of Mathematics Yearbooks. New York, 1926 – date.

Parke, N. G. *Guide to the Literature of Mathematics and Physics Including Related Works on Engineering Science.* 2nd ed., rev. New York, 1958.

Pervin, William J. *Foundations of General Topology.* New York, 1964.

Pontriagin, Lev S. *Foundations of Combinatorial Topology,* tr. F. Bagemihl, H. Komm, and W. Seidel. Rochester, N. Y., 1952.

——————. *Topological Groups,* tr. Emma Lehmer. Princeton, N. J., 1958.

Suppes, Patrick C. *Axiomatic Set Theory.* Princeton, N. J., 1960.

——————. *Introduction to Logic.* Princeton, N. J., 1958.

Journals

ACTA Mathematica (ACTA Math.)

American Journal of Mathematics (Am. J. Math.)

American Mathematical Monthly (Am. Math. Monthly)

American Mathematical Society, Bulletin (Am. Math. Soc. Bul.)

American Mathematical Society, Proceedings (Am. Math. Soc. Proc.)

American Mathematical Society, Transactions (Am. Math. Soc. Trans.)

Annals of Mathematics (Ann. of Math.)

Arithmetic Teacher

Duke Mathematics Journal (Duke Math. J.)

Duodecimal Bulletin (Duodecimal Bul.)

The Fibonacci Quarterly (Fibonacci Q.)

Journal of Algebra (J. Algebra)

Journal of Computer and Systems Sciences (J. Computer & Systems Sci.)

Journal of Mathematics and Physics (J. Math. & Phys.)

Journal of Research of the National Bureau of Standards (J. Res. Nat. Bur. Stand.)

Mathematical Review (Math. Rev.)

Mathematics Magazine (Math. Mag.)

Mathematics Teacher (Math. Teacher)

Philosophia Mathematica (Philos. Math.)

Proceedings of the Royal Society, Series A (Proc. Roy. Soc. Ser. A)

Quarterly Journal of Mathematics (Q. J. Math.)

Recreational Mathematics

Scripta Mathematica

SIAM Review

SRA "New" Mathematics Extension Services

SRA New Mathematics for Today's Teachers (K 6)

Updating Mathematics Services

PHOTOGRAPHY

Books

Abstracts of Photographic Science and Engineering Literature. New York, 1962–date.

Kodak Reference Handbook: Materials, Processes, Technique. Rochester, N.Y., 1940.

Photographic Abstracts. London, 1921–date.

Sowerby, A. L. M., ed. *Dictionary of Photography.* New York, 1956.

Stubbs, S. G. Blaxland, ed. *Modern Encyclopedia of Photography.* 2 vols. Boston, 1938.

Journals

Camera

International Photo Technik (Intern. Photo Technik)

Microcosm

Microdoc

National Professional Photographer

Photo Lab Index

PHYSICS

Books

Condon, Edward U., and Hugh Odishaw. *Handbook of Physics.* New York, 1958.

Glazebrook, Sir Richard T. *A Dictionary of Applied Physics.* 5 vols. New York, 1950.

Gray, Dwight E., et al. *American Institute of Physics Handbook.* 2nd ed. New York, 1963.

Gray, H. J., ed. *Dictionary of Physics.* London, 1958.

Weld, LeRoy D. *Glossary of Physics.* New York, 1937.

Journals

Advances in Physics (Advances in Phys.)

American Institute of Physics Newsletter (AIP Newsletter)

American Journal of Physics (Am. J. Phys.)

Annals of Physics (Ann. of Phys.)

JETP Letters

Journal of Applied Physics (J. Appl. Phys.)

Journal of Chemical Physics (J. Chem. Phys.)

Physical Review (Phys. Rev.)

Review of Modern Physics (Rev. Mod. Phys.)

Science Abstracts (Section A—Physics)

Art

Books

Adeline, Jules. *Adeline's Art Dictionary.* New York, 1927.

American Archives of World Art. *The American Library Compendium and Index of World Art.* New York, 1961.

American Art Annual. New York, 1898–date.

American Ceramic Society. *Ceramic Abstracts.* Easton, Pa., 1922–date.

Art Index. New York, 1929–date.

Boase, T. S. R., ed. *The Oxford History of English Art.* Oxford, 1949–. (In progress.)

Chamberlin, Mary W. *Guide to Art Reference Books.* Chicago, 1959.

Champlin, John D., and C. C. Perkins. *Cyclopedia of Painters and Paintings.* 4 vols. New York, 1886–1887.

Chase, George H., and C. R. Post. *A History of Sculpture.* New York, 1925.

Clapp, Jane. *Art Reproductions.* New York, 1961.

——————. *Museum Publications.* New York, 1962–date.

Encyclopedia of World Art. 15 vols. New York, 1959–date.

Fielding, Mantle. *Dictionary of American Painters, Sculptors and Engravers.* New York, 1945.

Gardner, Helen. *Art Through the Ages.* 4th ed. New York, 1959.

Gaunt, William. *Everyman's Dictionary of Pictorial Art.* 2 vols. New York, 1962.

Hammond, William A. *A Bibliography of Aesthetics and of the Philosophy of the Fine Arts from 1900 to 1932.* Rev. and enl. ed. New York, 1934.

Harper's Encyclopedia of Art. 2 vols. New York, 1937.

Herbert, Robert L. *Modern Artists on Art.* Englewood Cliffs, N.J., 1965.

The Index of Twentieth Century Artists. Vols. 1–4, no. 7; Oct. 1933–Apr. 1937. New York, 1933–1937.

Mallett, Daniel T. *Mallett's Index of Artists.* New York, 1935. Supplement, 1940.

McColvin, Eric R. *Painting: A Guide to the Best Books With Special Reference to the Requirements of Public Libraries.* London, 1934.

Monro, Isabel S., and Kate M. Monro. *Index to Reproductions of American Paintings.* New York, 1948.

—————— *Index to Reproductions of European Paintings.* New York, 1956.

Myers, Bernard S., ed. *Encyclopedia of Painting.* New York, 1955.

New York, Metropolitan Museum of Art. *Library Catalog.* 25 vols. Boston, 1960.

Pevsner, Nikolaus, ed. *The Pelican History of Art.* Baltimore, 1953–. (In progress.)

Pierson (Jr.), William Harvey, and M. Davidson, eds. *Arts of the United States: A Pictorial Survey.* New York, 1960.

The Praeger Picture Encyclopedia of Art. New York, 1958.

Read, Sir Herbert R. *A Concise History of Modern Painting.* London, 1962.

——————. *The Meaning of Art.* London, 1931.

Reinach, Salomon. *Apollo,* tr. F. Simmonds. New York, 1935.

Robb, David M., and J. J. Garrison. *Art in the Western World.* Rev. and enl. ed. New York, 1942.

Smith, Ralph C. *A Biographical Index of American Artists.* Baltimore, 1930.

Solon, Louis M. E. *Ceramic Literature.* London, 1910.

Special Libraries Association. Picture Division. *Picture Sources: An Introductory List,* ed. Helen Faye. New York, 1959.

Sturgis, Russell. *Annotated Bibliography of Fine Art: Painting, Sculpture, Architecture, Arts of Decoration and Illustration.* Boston, 1897.

Vance, Lucile E. *Illustration Index.* New York, 1957.

Who's Who in American Art. Washington, 1935–date.

Who's Who in Art. London, 1927–date.

Who's Who in Graphic Art, ed. Walter Amstutz. Zurich, 1962.

The Year's Art. London, 1880–date.

Journals

American Artist (Am. Artist)
Art Bulletin (Art Bul.)
Art Education (Art Ed.)
Art in Action
Art in America (Art in Am.)
Art Index
Art Journal (Art J.)
Art News (Art N.)
Artforum
Arts
Arts and Activities
Arts Yearbook
Connoisseur
Craft Horizons (Craft Horiz.)
Creative Crafts
Design
Design Quarterly (Design Q.)
Eastern
Everyday Art
Handweaver & Craftsman (Handweaver)
International Studio (Int. Studio)
Journal of Aesthetics and Art Criticism (J. Aesthetics)
Liturgical Arts (Liturg. Arts)
Magazine of Art (Mag. Art)
Motif
Portfolio
School Arts Book

School Arts Magazine (Sch. Arts Mag.)
Studies in Art Education (Stud. Art. Ed.)

Biological Sciences

Books

The American Yearbook: A Record of Events and Progress. New York, 1911–date.

Annotated Bibliography of Economic Geology. Lancaster, Pa., 1929–date.

Biological Abstracts. Menasha, Wis., 1926–date.

Blake, Sidney F. *Geographical Guide to Floras of the World: An Annotated List With Special Reference to Useful Plants and Common Plant Names.* Washington, D. C., 1942 – (In progress.)

California Academy of Sciences. *A Century of Progress in the Natural Sciences, 1853–1953.* San Francisco, 1955.

Cattell, J. McKeen, and Jacques Cattell, eds. *American Men of Science: A Biographical Directory.* 10th ed. Lancaster, Pa., 1906–date.

Comstock, Anna B. *Handbook of Nature-Study.* 24th ed. Ithaca, New York, 1939.

Gray, Henry. *Anatomy of the Human Body,* rev. C. M. Goss. 27th ed. Philadelphia, 1959.

Henderson, Isabella F., and W. D. Henderson. *Dictionary of Scientific Terms . . . in Biology, Botany, Zoology, Anatomy, Cytology, Genetics, Embryology, Physiology,* rev. J. H. Kenneth. 7th ed. Princeton, N. J., 1960.

Howard, A. V., ed. *Chambers's Dictionary of Scientists.* New York, 1951.

Jacobs, Morris B., et al. *Dictionary of Microbiology.* Princeton, N. J., 1957.

Jenkins, Frances B. *Science Reference Sources.* 4th ed. Champaign, Ill., 1965.

Palmer, Ephraim L. *Fieldbook of Natural History.* New York, 1949.

Sarton, George. *Introduction to the History of Science.* Baltimore, 1927–1948.

Science Abstracts. London, 1898–date.

Smith, R. C. *Guide to the Literature of the Zoological Sciences.* 5th ed. Minneapolis, 1958.

Spector, William S. *Handbook of Biological Data.* Philadelphia, 1956.

Stedman, T. L. *Stedman's Medical Dictionary.* 18th ed., rev. Baltimore, 1953.

U. S. Department of the Interior, Bureau of Mines. *Minerals Yearbook.* Washington, D.C., 1933–date.

Van Nostrand's Scientific Encyclopedia. 3rd ed. Princeton, N. J., 1958.

Willis, J. C. *Dictionary of the Flowering Plants and Ferns.* 6th ed., rev. Cambridge, 1931.

World Medical Association. *Seventy-Five Years of Medical Progress, 1878–1953.* Philadelphia, 1954.

Journals

Advancement of Science

Advances in Botanical Research (Advances Botan. Res.)

Advancing Frontiers of Plant Sciences

American Journal of Anatomy (Am. J. Anat.)

American Journal of Botany (Am. J. Botany)

American Journal of Physiology (Am. J. Physiol.)

American Scientist (Am. Scientist)

Animal Behavior

Annales de l'Institut Pasteur

Annals and Magazine of Natural History (Ann. & Mag. Nat. Hist.)

Annals of Botany (Ann. Botany)

Annals of the Missouri Botanical Garden (Ann. Mo. Botan. Garden)

Applied Microbiology (Appl. Microbiol.)

Archiv für Hydrobiologie

Archives of Biochemistry and Biophysics (Arch. Biochem. & Biophys.)

Audubon Field Notes

Audubon Magazine

Bacteriological Reviews (Bacteriol. Rev.)

Biochemical and Biophysical Research Commission (Biochem. & Biophys. Research Comm.)

Biochemistry (Biochem.)

Biochemistry Journal (Biochem. J.)

Biochimica et Biophysica Acta

Biological Abstracts (Biol. Abstr.)

Bioscience

Botanical Review (Botan. Rev.)

Bulletin of Aquatic Biology (Bull. Aquatic Biol.)

Bulletin of Experimental Biology and Medicine (Bull. Exptl. Biol. & Med.)

Bulletin of the Atomic Scientists (Bull. Atomic Scientists)

Canadian Journal of Botany (Canadian J. Botany.)

Canadian Journal of Microbiology (Canadian J. Microbiol.)

Current Contents

DOKLADY – Biochemistry section

DOKLADY – Biological Sciences section

DOKLADY – Botanical Sciences section

Ecology

Evolution
Experimental Cell Research (Exptl. Cell
Research)
Federation Proceedings (Federation Proc.)
General Science Quarterly (Gen. Sci.
Quart.)
Genetics
Geological Society of America—Bulletin
(Geol. Soc. Am. Bull.)
Geophysical Abstracts (Geophys. Abstr.)
Heredity
Herpetologica
Human Genetics
Hydrobiologica
International Abstracts of Biological Sci-
ences (Intern. Abstr. Biol. Sci.)
International Bureau for Plant Taxonomy
(Intern. Bur. Plant. Taxonomy)
Journal of Animal Behavior (J. Animal
Behavior)
Journal of Animal Ecology (J. Animal
Ecology)
Journal of Bacteriology (J. Bacteriol.)
Journal of Biological Chemistry (J. Biol.
Chem.)
Journal of Cellular and Comparative Physi-
ology (J. Cellular & Comp. Physiol.)
Journal of Clinical Investigation (J. Clin.
Invest.)
Journal of Ecology (J. Ecol.)
Journal of Experimental Biology (J. Exptl.
Biol.)
Journal of Experimental Medicine (J.
Exptl. Med.)
Journal of Experimental Zoology (J. Exptl.
Zool.)
Journal of General Microbiology (J. Gen.
Microbiol.)
Journal of Geology (J. Geol.)
Journal of Immunology (J. Immunol.)
Journal of Lipid Research (J. Lipid Re-
search)
Journal of Mammology (J. Mammol.)
Journal of Molecular Biology (J. Molecular
Biol.)
Journal of Paleontology (J. Paleontol.)
Journal of Physiology (J. Physiol.)
Journal of Protozoology (J. Protozool.)
Journal of Wildlife Management (J. Wildl.
Mgmt.)
Linnean Society of London Journal (Lin-
nean Soc. London J.)
Mutation Research
National Academy of Sciences—Proceed-
ings (Proc. Nat. Acad. Sci.)
National Wildlife (Nat. Wildl.)
Naturalist
Nature

New York Academy of Sciences, Annals of
(Ann. NY Acad. Sci.)
Palaeobotanist
Philosophy of Science
Physiological Reviews (Physiol. Rev.)
Physiological Zoology (Physiol. Zool.)
Plant Physiology (Plant Physiol.)
Plant World
Proceedings of the National Academy of
Science (Proc. Nat. Acad. Sci.)
Radiation Research (Radiation Res.)
Review of Applied Mycology (Rev. Appl.
Mycology)
Science
Science Education (Sci. Ed.)
Scientific American (Sci. Am.)
Scientific American Monthly (Sci. Am.
Monthly)
Scientific Monthly (Sci. Monthly)
Soil Conservation (Soil Conserv.)
Stain Technology
Zeitschrift für Zellforschung und mikro-
skopische Anatomie

Business

Books

Brown, Stanley M., ed. *Business Executive's
Handbook,* rev. Lillian Doris. 4th ed. New
York, 1953.
Business Periodicals Index. New York, 1958—
date.

> A subject index to 128 business
> periodicals, including many for-
> merly indexed in *Industrial Arts
> Index.*

Clark, Donald T., and Bert A. Gottfried.
Dictionary of Business and Finance. New
York, 1957.
Coman, Edwin T. *Sources of Business Infor-
mation.* Rev. ed. Berkeley, Calif., 1964.
Harvard University Graduate School of
Business Administration. *A Classification
of Business Literature.* Rev. ed. Hamden,
Conn., 1961.
Horton, Byrne J., et al. *Dictionary of Modern
Economics.* Washington, D.C., 1948.

> Deals with important factors af-
> fecting economics, including Su-
> preme Court decisions.

Lazarus, Harold. *American Business Dictionary.* New York, 1957.
Munn, G. G., ed. *Encyclopedia of Banking
and Finance,* rev. Ferdinand L. Garcia.
6th ed. Boston, 1962.
Nemmers, Erwin E., and C. C. Janzen, eds.

Dictionary of Economics and Business. Paterson, N. J., 1959.

Prentice-Hall Editorial Staff. *Encyclopedic Dictionary of Real Estate Practice.* Rev. ed. Englewood Cliffs, N. J., 1962.

Winser, Marian (Manley). *Business Information: How To Find and Use It.* New York, 1955.

Journals

Accountants' Digest (Account. Dig.)
Accounting Research (Account. Res.)
Accounting Review (Accounting R.)
Appraisal Journal (Appraisal J.)
Barron's National Business and Financial Weekly (Barrons)
Better Living
Business Horizons (Bsns. Horizons)
Business Week (Bsns. W.)
Changing Times
Consumers' Research Bulletin (Consumers' Res. Bul.)
Dun's Review and Modern Industry (Duns R. & Mod. Ind.)
Economic Indicators (Econ. Indicators)
Employment Security Review (Employment Security Rev.)
Factory Management and Maintenance (Factory Mgt. & Maintenance)
Federal Reserve Bulletin (Fed. Res. Bul.)
Federal Tax Articles (Fed. Tax Articles)
Federal Tax Guide (Fed. Tax Guide)
Financial Executive (Fin. Exec.)
Fortune
Harvard Business Review (Harvard Bsns. R.)
Human Engineering (Human Eng.)
Journal of Accountancy (J. Account.)
Journal of Finance (J. Finance)
Journal of Insurance Information (J. Ins. Information)
Journal of Marketing (J. Mktg.)
Journal of Retailing (J. Retailing)
Kiplinger Washington Letter
Labor Market and Employment Security
Lloyd's Bank Review (Lloyd's Bank Rev.)
Magazine of Wallstreet and Business Analyst (Mag. Wall. St.)
Management Accounting (Mgt. Account.)
Management News (Mgt. News)
Management Review (Mgt. R.)
Monthly Review (Monthly Rev.)
Moody's Banks and Finance
Moody's Handbook of Widely Held Common Stocks
Moody's Industrials
Moody's Magazine
Nation's Business (Nation's Bsns.)
Office Executive

Over-the-Counter Securities Review
Personnel and Guidance Journal (Personnel & Guidance J.)
Personnel Psychology
Sales Management (Sales Mgt.)
Social Security Bulletin (Soc. Sec. Bul.)
Standard and Poor s Corporation Records
Supervisory Management (Supervisory Mgt.)
Survey of Current Business (Survey Cur. Bsns.)
Systems
Tax Executive
Value Line
Wall Street Journal (Wall St. J.)

Education

Books

Alexander, Carter, and A. J. Burke. *How to Locate Educational Information and Data.* 4th ed. New York, 1958.

American Council on Education. *American Universities and Colleges.* Washington, 1928–date.

Biography Index. New York, 1946–date.

Buros, O. K. *Mental Measurements Yearbook.* New Brunswick, 1938–date.

Dissertation Abstracts. Ann Arbor, Mich., 1938–date.

Education Abstracts. Vols. 1–9. Fulton, Mo., 1936–1944.

The Education Index. New York, 1929–1964.
A cumulative author and subject index to a selected list of educational periodicals, books, and pamphlets.

Educational Film Guide. New York, 1936–1962.

Good, Carter V., ed. *Dictionary of Education.* 2nd ed. New York, 1959.

International Yearbook of Education. 10th ed. Geneva, 1948.

Monroe, Paul, ed. *A Cyclopedia of Education.* 5 vols. New York, 1911–1913.
Valuable for its presentation of the history and philosophy of education.

Monroe, Walter S., ed. *Encyclopedia of Educational Research: A Project of the American Educational Research Association.* 3rd ed. New York, 1960.

—————, and Louis Shores, comps. *Bibliographies and Summaries in Education to July 1935.* New York, 1936.

Public Affairs Information Service. New York, 1915–date.
Especially valuable for material on educational legislation, recent government publications, and bulletins on school administration.

UNESCO. *World Survey of Education.* 3 vols. Paris, 1955–date.

U.S. Office of Education. *Diennial Survey of Education.* Washington, D.C., 1916/1918–date.

Who's Who In American Education. New York, 1928–date.

Yearbook of Education. London, 1932-date.

Journals

American School Board Journal (Am. Sch. Board J.)

Bulletin of the National Association of Secondary School Principals (Bul. Nat. Assn. Sec. Sch. Principals)

Childhood Education (Childh. Ed.)

Educational Forum (Ed. Forum)

Educational Leadership (Ed. Leadership)

Elementary School Journal (El. Sch. J.)

Elementary School Teacher (El. Sch. Teach.)

Future Teacher (Future Teach.)

Harvard Educational Review (Harvard Ed. R.)

Journal of Educational Research (J. Ed. Res.)

Journal of Experimental Education (J. Exp. Ed.)

Journal of Higher Education (J. Higher Ed.)

Journal of Secondary Education (J. Sec. Ed.)

Journal of Teacher Education (J. Teach. Ed.)

Junior College Journal (Jun. Col. J.)

National Elementary Principal (Nat. El. Prin.)

NEA Journal (NEA J.)

NEA Research Bulletin (NEA Res. Bul.)

Review of Educational Research (R. Ed. Res.)

School Executive (Sch. Exec.)

School Life (Sch. Life)

Teachers College Journal (Teach. Col. J.)

English Language and Literature

Books

Abstracts of English Studies. Boulder, Colo., 1958–date.

Arms, George, and Joseph M. Kuntz. *Poetry Explication: A Checklist of Interpretations Since 1925 of British and American Poems Past and Present.* Denver, 1962.

Baker, Ernest A. *The History of the English Novel.* 10 vols. New York, 1961–1964.

Baldensperger, Fernand, and Werner P. Friederich. *Bibliography of Comparative Literature.* 3rd ed. New York, 1960.

Bateson, F. W., ed. *Cambridge Bibliography of English Literature.* 4 vols. New York, 1941–date.

Baugh, Albert C., ed. *A Literary History of England.* London, 1948.

Bell, Inglis F., and Donald Baird. *The English Novel, 1578–1956: A Checklist of Twentieth-Century Criticisms.* Denver, 1959.

Bernhardt, William F., ed. *Granger's Index to Poetry.* 5th ed., rev. and enl. New York, 1962.

Blanck, Jacob. *Bibliography of American Literature.* New Haven, 1955– .
   In progress: Vol. IV to Joseph Holt Ingraham, 1959.

Bond, Donald F. *A Reference Guide to English Studies.* Chicago, 1962.
   A revision of the *Bibliographical Guide to English Studies* by Tom Peete Cross.

Bruncken, Herbert. *Subject Index to Poetry.* Chicago, 1940.

Cambridge History of American Literature. 4 vols. New York, 1933.

Cambridge History of English Literature. New York, 1939.

Cook, Dorothy E., and Isabel S. Monro. *Short Story Index.* New York, 1953–date.

Courthope, William J. *A History of English Poetry.* 6 vols. New York, 1895–1910.

Craigie, Sir William, and James R. Hulbert. *A Dictionary of American English on Historical Principles.* 4 vols. Chicago, 1936–1944.

Diehl, Katharine S. *Religions, Mythologies, Folklores: An Annotated Bibliography.* 2nd ed. New York, 1962.

Eastman, Mary Huse. *Index to Fairy Tales, Myths, and Legends.* 2nd ed., rev. Boston, 1926. Supplement, 1937.

Ebisch, Walther, and Levin L. Schücking. *A Shakespeare Bibliography.* Oxford, 1931. Supplement, 1937.

English Association. *The Year's Work in English Studies.* Oxford, 1919–1921–date.

Gohdes, Clarence. *Bibliographical Guide to the Study of the Literature of the U.S.A.* 2nd ed. Durham, N.C., 1963.

Gray, Louis H., and John A. Macculloch, eds. *Mythology of All Races.* 13 vols. Boston, 1916–1964.

Hart, James D. *The Oxford Companion to American Literature.* 4th ed., rev. and enl. New York, 1965.

Harvey, Sir Paul. *The Oxford Companion to Classical Literature.* 3rd ed. Oxford, 1940.

——————. *The Oxford Companion to English Literature.* 3rd ed. Oxford, 1946.

——————, and Janet E. Heseltine. *The Oxford Companion to French Literature.* Oxford, 1959.

Haywood, Charles. *A Bibliography of North American Folklore and Folksong.* 2nd ed., rev. New York, 1961.

Hornstein, Lillian H., ed. *Reader's Companion to World Literature.* New York, 1956.

Jones, Howard Mumford. *Guide to American Literature and Its Backgrounds Since 1890.* 3rd rev. ed. Cambridge, Mass., 1964.

Kennedy, Arthur G., and Donald B. Sands. *A Concise Bibliography for Students of English.* 4th ed. Stanford, Calif., 1960.

Kunitz, Stanley J., and Howard Haycraft, eds. *American Authors, 1600–1900.* New York, 1938.

———. *British Authors Before 1800.* New York, 1952.

———. *British Authors of the Nineteenth Century.* New York, 1936.

———. *The Junior Book of Authors.* 2nd rev. ed. New York, 1951.

———. *Twentieth Century Authors.* New York, 1942. Supplement, 1955.

Larousse Encyclopedia of Mythology. London, 1959.

Leary, Lewis. *Articles on American Literature Appearing in Current Periodicals, 1900–50.* Durham, N.C., 1954.

Magill, Frank N., ed. *Masterplots.* 6 vols. New York, 1960.

Modern Humanities Research Association. *Annual Bibliography of English Language and Literature, 1920–.* New York, 1920–1921–date.

Morgan, Bayard Q. *A Critical Bibliography of German Literature in English Translation, 1481–1927.* 2nd ed. New York, 1965.

Nyren, Dorothy, ed. *A Library of Literary Criticism: Modern American Literature.* New York, 1960.

Richards, Robert F., ed. *Concise Dictionary of American Literature.* New York, 1955.

Sampson, George, ed. *The Concise Cambridge Bibliography of English Literature.* Cambridge, 1961.

Sell, Violet, et al. *Subject Index to Poetry for Children and Young People.* Chicago, 1957.

Shipley, Joseph T., ed. *Dictionary of World Literature.* New York, 1943.

Smith, Horatio, ed. *Columbia Dictionary of Modern European Literature.* New York, 1947.

Spiller, Robert E., et al. *Literary History of the United States.* 3rd ed. New York, 1964.

Steinberg, S. H., ed. *Cassell's Encyclopaedia of Literature.* 2 vols. London, 1953.

Tate, Allen, *Sixty American Poets, 1896–1944.* Rev. ed. Washington, D.C., 1954.

Taylor, Archer, and Bartlett J. Whiting, comps. *A Dictionary of American Proverbs and Proverbial Phrases, 1820–80.* Cambridge, Mass., 1958.

Thompson, Stith. *Motif-Index of Folk Literature: A Classification of Narrative Elements in Folktales, Ballads, Myths, Fables, Mediaeval Romances . . .* Rev. and enl. ed. 6 vols. Bloomington, Ind., 1955–1958.

Thrall, William F., and Addison Hibbard, eds. *A Handbook to Literature,* rev. and enl. by C. Hugh Holman. New York, 1960.

Wilson, Frank P., and Bonamy Dobree, eds. *The Oxford History of English Literature.* New York, 1945–. (In progress.)

Woodress, James L. *Dissertations in American Literature, 1891–1961.* Durham, N. C., 1962.

Journals

Abstracts of English Studies
American Journal of Philology (AJPh)
American Literature (AL)
American Notes & Queries (AN&Q)
American Quarterly (AQ)
American Scholar (ASch)
American Speech (AS)
College Composition and Communication (CCC)
College English (CE)
Comparative Literature (CL)
English Language Notes (ELN)
English Literary History, Journal of (ELH)
English Studies (ES)
Explicator (Expl)
Journal of English and Germanic Philology (JEGP)
Modern Drama (MD)
Modern Fiction Studies (MFS)
Modern Language Abstracts
Modern Language Forum
Modern Language Journal (MLJ)
Modern Language Notes (MLN)
Modern Language Quarterly (MLQ)
Modern Language Review (MLR)
Modern Philology (MP)
New England Quarterly (NEQ)
Nineteenth Century Fiction (NCF)
Philological Quarterly (PQ)
PMLA (PMLA is the title.)
Renaissance News (RN)
Review of English Studies (RES)
Romance Philology (RPh)
Shakespeare Quarterly (SQ)
Studies in Philology (SP)
Victorian Studies (VS)

Foreign Languages

FRENCH

Books

Bornecque, Pierre, and Jacques-Henry. *La France et sa littérature: Guide complet dans le cadre de la civilisation mondiale.* France, 1953.

Castex, P., and P. Surer. *Manuel des études littéraires françaises.* Paris, 1953.

Duby, Georges, and Robert Mandrou. *A History of French Civilization.* New York, 1964.

Grevisse, Maurice. *Le Bon Usage: Grammaire française.* Paris, 1961.

Lagarde, André, and Laurent Michard. *Collection literaire: Texts et littératures.* 6 vols. Paris, 1961.

Lanson, G., and P. Tuffrau. *Manuel illustré d'histoire de la littérature française.* Paris, 1953.

Lévêque, André. *Histoire de la civilisation française.* New York, 1965.

Mansion, J. E. *Concise French and English Dictionary.* Boston, 1949.

──────. *Heath's Standard French and English Dictionary.* New York, 1934.

Maurois, André. *A History of France,* trans. H. L. Binsse and Gerard Hopkins. London, 1950.

Miller, Minnie, James R. Nielson, and Jean Leblon. *Précis de civilisation française.* New York, 1966.

Nouveau Larousse Classique. 3rd ed. Paris, 1959.

Petit Larousse. Paris, 1962.

Journals

The French Review (FR)

Realities

GERMAN

Books

Betteridge, Harold T. *The New Cassell's German Dictionary.* New York, 1958.

Brenner, Emil. *Deutsche Literaturgeschichte.* 15th ed. Wünsiedel, 1960.

Bruhns, Leo. *Deutsche Künstler in Selbstdarstellungen.* Königstein im Taurus, 1957.

Bruns, Friedrich. *Die Lese der deutschen Lyrik von Klopstock bis Rilke.* New York, 1938.

Der Sprach-Brockhaus. 7th ed. Wiesbaden, 1961.

Fleissner, O. S., and E. M. Fleissner. *Deutsches Literatur-Lesebuch.* 3rd ed. New York, 1959.

Krell, Leo, and Leonhard Fiedler. *Deutsche Literaturgeschichte.* 8th ed. Bamberg, 1960.

Lennartz, Franz. *Dichter und Schriftsteller unserer Zeit.* Stuttgart, 1959.

Loram, Ian C., and Leland R. Phelps. *Aus unserer Zeit: Dichter des zwanzigsten Jahrhunderts.* New York, 1956.

Martini, Fritz. *Deutsche Literatur Geschichte von den Anfängen bis zur Gewenwart.* Stuttgart, 1960.

Mathieu, Gustave, and Guy Stern. *Brieflich Erzählt.* New York, 1956.

Richter, Karl. *Deutsche Heldensagen.* München, 1957.

Rose, Ernst. *A History of German Literature.* New York, 1960.

Scherer, George A. C. *Selected German Ballads.* Boston, 1951.

Zucker, A. E. *Amerika und Deutschland.* New York, 1953.

Journals

The German Quarterly (GQ)

Merian: Das Monatsheft der Städte und Landschaften

Der Spiegel

RUSSIAN

Books

Blinoff, Marthe. *Life and Thought in Old Russia.* University Park, Penn., 1961.

Morison, Walter A. *Studies in Russian Forms and Uses.* London, 1959.

Muller, V. K. *English-Russian Dictionary.* New York, 1959.

Rauch, Georg von. *History of Soviet Russia.* New York, 1957.

Treadgold, Donald W. *Twentieth Century Russia.* 2nd ed. New York, 1964.

Journals

The Russian Review (Rus. R.)

Slavic Review (Slav. R.)

SPANISH

Books

Anderson Imbert, Enrique. *Historia do la literatura hispanoamericana.* Mexico City, 1961.

──────, and Eugenio Floeit. *Literatura hispanoamericana.* New York, 1960.

Augé, C. Y. P., and Miguel do Toro y Gisbert. *Pequeño Larousse Ilustrado.* New York, 1961.

Cuyás, Arturo. *Appleton's Revised English-Spanish and Spanish-English Dictionary.* 4th ed. New York, 1960.

Eoff, Sherman H. *The Modern Spanish Novel.* New York, 1961.

Flores, Angel, ed. *Historia y antologia del*

cuento y la novela en Hispanoamerica. New York, 1959.

García López, José. *Historia de la literatura española.* 4th ed. New York, 1963.

González López, Emilio. *Historia de la civilización española.* New York, 1959.

Hamilton, Carlos D. *Historia de la literatura hispanoamericana.* New York, 1960–1961.

Hespelt, E. Herman, et al. *An Anthology of Spanish American Literature.* New York, 1946.

Northrup, George Tyler. *An Introduction to Spanish Literature.* Chicago, 1960.

Pattison, Walter T., ed. *Representative Spanish Authors.* New York, 1942.

Romera-Navarro, Miguel. *Historia de la Literatura Española.* 2nd ed. Boston, 1949.

Torrente Ballester, G. *Literatura Española Contemporánea.* Madrid, 1949.

Velázquez de la Cadena, Mariano, et al. *New Revised Velázquez Spanish and English Dictionary.* Chicago, 1960.

Journals
Hispania
Hispanic Review (HR)
Visión: Revista Internacional

Health and Physical Education

Books

American Association for Health, Physical Education, and Recreation. *Research Methods in Health, Physical Education, Recreation,* ed. M. Gladys Scott. Washington, D.C., 1959.

Avis, Frederick Compton. *The Sportsman's Glossary.* London, 1961.

Bucher, Charles A. *Foundations of Physical Education.* 3rd ed. St. Louis, 1960.
Bibliography provided at the end of every chapter.

Bunn, John W. *Scientific Principles of Coaching.* Englewood Cliffs, N. J., 1962.

Chujoy, Anatole. *The Dance Encyclopedia.* New York, 1949.

Cooper, John M., and Ruth B. Glassow. *Kinesiology.* St. Louis, 1963.

Cummings, Parke. *The Dictionary of Sports.* New York, 1949.

Dalen, Deobold B., et al. *A World History of Physical Education.* New York, 1953.

Greenwood, Frances A. *Bibliography of Swimming.* New York, 1940.

Guide to Dance Periodicals. 10 vols. Gainesville, Fla., 1931/35–1964.

Higginson, A. Henry. *British and American Sporting Authors, Their Writings and Biographies.* Berryville, Va., 1949.

Johnson, W. R. *Science and Medicine of Exercise and Sports.* New York, 1960.
A handbook including bibliography.

Lovell, Eleanor C., and Ruth M. Hall. *Index to Handicrafts, Modelmaking, and Workshop Projects.* Boston, 1936. Supplements, 1943, 1950.

Magriel, Paul David. *A Bibliography of Dancing.* New York, 1936. 4th supplement, 1941.

Menke, Frank G. *The Encyclopedia of Sports.* 2nd rev. ed. New York, 1960.

Minneapolis Public Library. Music Dept. *Index to Folk Dances and Singing Games.* Chicago, 1936. Supplement, 1949.

Moomaw, Virginia. *Dance Research.* Washington, D.C., 1958.

National Recreation Association. *Guide to Books on Recreation.* Washington, D.C., 1959–date.
Also published as Part 2 of the Sept. issue of *Recreation.*

Neumeyer, M. H., and E. S. Neumeyer. *Leisure and Recreation.* 3rd ed. New York, 1958.
Contains chapter bibliographies.

Spalding's Official Athletic Almanac. New York, 1893–date.

Weston, Arthur. *The Making of American Physical Education.* New York, 1962.

Williams, Jesse Feiring. *The Principles of Physical Education.* Philadelphia, 1964.

Wohlford, Mildred. *Bowling-Fencing-Golf Guide.* Washington, D.C., 1958.

Journals
American Journal of Public Health and the Nation's Health
American Recreation Journal (Am. Rec. J.)
American Recreation Society Newsletter (ARS Newsletter)
Aquatic Artist
Athletic Journal (Athl. J.)
Ballroom Dance Magazine (Ballroom Dance Mag.)
Collegiate Baseball (Col. Baseball)
Dance Magazine (Dance Mag.)
Dance Observer (Dance Obs.)
Dance Perspectives (Dance Persp.)
Dance Scope
Field and Stream (Field & S.)
Health Bulletin (Health Bul.)
Health, Education, and Welfare Indicators (Health, Ed. & Welf. Indicators)

Health, Education and Welfare Trends (Health Ed. & Welf. Trends)
Hygeia
Hygiene and Physical Education (Hygiene & Phys. Ed.)
Journal of Health and Physical Education (J. Health & Phys. Ed.)
Journal of Health, Physical Education and Recreation (J. Health, Phys. Ed. & Rec.)
Journal of Hygiene (J. Hygiene)
Journal of School Health (J. Sch. Health)
Modern Gymnast (Mod. Gymnast)
Playground
Public Health Reports
Outdoor Life
Outing
Recreation
Research Quarterly of AAHPER
Scholastic Coach (Schol. Coach)
Sports Illustrated (Sports Illus.)
Today's Health
Track and Field News (Track & Field N.)
World Health
World Tennis

Home Economics

CHILD DEVELOPMENT

Books

Almy, Millie Corinne. *Child Development*. New York, 1955.
Breckenridge, Marian E., and Margaret Nesbitt Murphy. *Growth and Development of the Young Child*. 7th ed. Philadelphia, 1963.
Crow, Lester D., and Alice Crow. *Child Development and Adjustment*. New York, 1962.
Jersild, Arthur T. *Child Psychology*. 4th ed. New York, 1954.
Langford, Louise M. *Guidance of the Young Child*. New York, 1960.
Stone, Lawrence Joseph, and Joseph Church. *Childhood and Adolescence*. New York, 1957.

CLOTHING
Books
Bane, Allyne. *Creative Sewing*. New York, 1956.
Brockman, Helen L. *Theory of Fashion Design*. New York, 1965.
Chambers, Helen G., and Verna Moulton. *Clothing Selection*. Philadelphia, 1961.
Erwin, Mabel D., and Lila A. Kinchen.

Clothing for Moderns. 3rd ed. New York, 1957.
Evans, Mary. *Costume Throughout the Ages*. 3rd ed. Philadelphia, 1950.
Hansen, Henry Harold. *Costumes and Styles*. New York, 1956.
Hillhouse, Marion S. *Dress Selection and Design*. New York, 1963.
Hollen, Norma R. *Flat Pattern Methods*. Minneapolis, 1965.
————————, and Jane Saddler. *Textiles*. 2nd ed. New York, 1963.
Monro, Isabel Stevenson, and Kate M. Monro. *Costume Index*. New York, 1957.
Norris, Herbert. *Costume and Fashion*. 6 vols. London, 1925–1933.
Roach, Mary Ellen, and Joanne Bubolz Eicher. *Dress, Adornment and the Social Order*. New York, 1965.
Stout, Evelyn E. *Introduction to Textiles*. 2nd ed. New York, 1965.
Tate, Mildred T., and Oris Glisson. *Family Clothing*. New York, 1961.
Wingate, Isabel B. *Textile Fabrics and Their Selection*. 5th ed. Englewood Cliffs, N. J., 1955.

Journals
Harper's Bazaar
Mademoiselle (Mlle.)
Seventeen
Vogue
Vogue Pattern Book

CONSUMER ECONOMICS

Books
Gordon, Leland J. *Economics for Consumers*. 4th ed. New York, 1961.
Hamilton, David. *The Consumer in Our Economy*. Boston, 1962.
Mann, George C. *Bibliography on Consumer Education* New York, 1939.
Troelstrup, Archie W. *Consumer Problems and Personal Finance*. 3rd ed. New York, 1965.

Journals
Consumer
Consumer Bulletin (Consumer Bul.)
Consumer Reports (Consumer Rep.)
Family Economic Review (Family Econ. Rev.)
Forecast for Home Economics (Forecast Home Econ.)
Home Progress
Home Science Magazine (Home Sci. Mag.)
Journal of Home Economics (J. Home Economics)

Journal of Marriage and the Family (J. Marriage and the Family)
Practical Home Economics (Practical Home Econ.)

EQUIPMENT
Books
Ehrenkranz, Florence, and Lydia Inman. *Equipment in the Home.* 2nd ed. New York, 1966.
Johnston, Betty Jane. *Equipment for Modern Living.* New York, 1965.
Peet, Louise J., and Lenore S. Thye. *Household Equipment.* 5th ed. New York, 1961.
Van Zante, Helen J. *Household Equipment Principles.* Englewood Cliffs, N. J., 1964.

FAMILY LIVING

Books
Bell, Robert R. *Marriage and Family Interaction.* Homewood, Ill., 1963.
Bowman, Henry A. *Marriage for Moderns.* 5th ed. New York, 1965.
Burgess, Ernest W., Paul Wallin, and Gladys Denny Schultz. *Engagement and Marriage.* Philadelphia, 1953.
Landis, Judson T., and Mary G. Landis. *Building a Successful Marriage.* 4th ed. Englewood Cliffs, N. J., 1963.
Landis, Paul H. *Making the Most of Marriage.* 3rd ed. New York, 1965.

HOMEMAKING EDUCATION

Books
Hall, Olive A., and Beatrice Paolucci. *Teaching Home Economics.* New York, 1961.
Roberts, Roy W. *Vocational and Practical Arts Education.* New York, 1965.
Williamson, Maude, and Mary Lyle. *Homemaking Education in the High School.* 4th ed. New York, 1961.

INTERIOR DECORATION

Books
Faulkner, Ray, and S. Faulkner. *Inside Today's Home.* Rev. ed. New York, 1960.
Rogers, Kate E. *Modern House, U.S.A.* New York, 1962.
Whiton, Sherrill. *Elements of Interior Design and Decoration.* 3rd ed. Philadelphia, 1964.

Journals
American Home (Am. Home)
Better Homes and Gardens (Bet. Hom. & Gard.)

House and Garden (House & Gard.)
House Beautiful (House B.)
Interiors

MANAGEMENT
Books
Goodyear, Margaret R., and Mildred Chapin Klohr. *Managing for Effective Living.* 2nd ed. New York, 1965.
Gross, Irma H., and Elizabeth Crandall. *Management for Modern Families.* New York, 1954.

NUTRITION
Books
Chaney, Margaret S., and Margaret L. Ross. *Nutrition.* 7th ed. Boston, 1966.
Graves, Lulu G., and Clarence W. Taber. *A Dictionary of Food and Nutrition.* Philadelphia, 1938.
Hughes, Osee. *Introductory Foods.* 4th ed. New York, 1962.
Justin, Margaret M., Lucile Osborn Rust, and Gladys E. Vail. *Foods.* 4th ed. Boston, 1956.
Kleiner, Israel S., and James M. Orten. *Biochemistry.* 6th ed. St. Louis, 1962.
Martin, Ethel Austin. *Nutrition in Action.* 2nd ed. New York, 1965.
Proudfit, Fairfax T. *Normal and Therapeutic Nutrition.* 12th ed. New York, 1961.
Wilson, Eva D., Katherine H. Fisher, and Mary E. Fuqua. *Principles of Nutrition.* 2nd ed. New York, 1965.

Journals
American Journal of Clinical Nutrition (Am. J. Clinical Nutrition)
Institutions Magazine (Institutions Mag.)
Journal of Food Science (J. Food Science)
Journal of Nutrition (J. Nutrition)
Journal of the American Dietetic Association (J. Am. Dietetic Assn.)

Music
Books
Apel, Willi. *Harvard Dictionary of Music.* Cambridge, Mass., 1947.
——————, and Ralph T. Daniel. *The Harvard Brief Dictionary of Music.* Cambridge, Mass., 1960.
Baker, Theodore. *Baker's Biographical Dictionary of Musicians.* 4th ed., rev. and enl. New York, 1940.

. *Biographical Dictionary of Musicians,* rev. Nicolas Slonimsky. 5th ed. New York, 1958.

—————. *Dictionary of Musical Terms.* New York, 1923.

Bessaraboff, Nicholas. *Ancient European Musical Instruments.* Boston, 1941.

Carter, Henry Holland. *A Dictionary of Middle English Musical Terms,* ed. George B. Gerhard et al. Bloomington, Ind., 1961.

Chase, Gilbert. *A Guide to Latin American Music.* Library of Congress, Music Division, Latin American Series No. 5. Washington, D. C., 1945.

Clement, Felix, and Pierre Larousse. *Dictionnaire des Opéras (Dictionnaire Lyrique).* Paris, 1897.

Clough, Francis F., and G. J. Cuming. *The World's Encyclopaedia of Recorded Music.* London, 1952.

Dictionary of Modern Music and Musicians. London, 1924.

Einstein, Alfred. *Music in the Romantic Era.* New York, 1947.

Eitner, Robert. *Biographisch-Bibliographisches Quellen-Lexikon der Musiker und Musikgelehrten der Christlichen Zeitrechnung Bis Zur Mitte Des Neunzehnten Jahrhunderts.* 10 vols. Leipzig, 1900–1904.

Ewen, David. *American Composers Today.* New York, 1949.

—————. *Encyclopedia of Concert Music.* New York, 1959.

Fetis, Francois Joseph. *Biographie Universelle des Musiciens et Bibliographie Générale de la Musique.* 2nd ed. 8 vols. Paris, 1866–1868.

Grove, Sir George. *Grove's Dictionary of Music and Musicians,* ed. H. C. Colles. 3rd ed. 5 vols. London, 1927–1928.

—————. *Grove's Dictionary of Music and Musicians,* ed. Eric Blom. 5th ed. 10 vols. London, 1954–1961.

Handbuch der Musikwissenschaft, ed. Ernest Bücken. 13 vols. New York, 1949–1950.

Haydon, Glen. *Introduction to Musicology.* New York, 1941.

Hewitt, Helen. *Doctoral Dissertations in Musicology.* 4th ed. Philadelphia, 1965.

Heyer, Anna Harriet. *A Check-List of Publications of Music.* Ann Arbor, Mich., 1944.

Hofmeister, Adolph. *Hofmeisters Handbuch der Musikliteratur.* 3 vols. Leipzig, 1844–1845.

Howard, John Tasker. *The World's Great*

Operas. Newly enl. ed. New York, 1959.

Keohn, Ernst C. "The Bibliography of Music," *Musical Quarterly,* V (1919), 231–254.

King, Alexander Hyatt. "Recent Work in Music Bibliography," *The Library,* XXVI, Sept.–Dec., 1945.

Kobbé, Gustav. *Complete Opera Book,* ed. the Earl of Harewood. New York, 1963.

Kolodin, Irving. *New Guide to Recorded Music.* New York, 1947.

Láng, Paul Henry. *Music in Western Civilization.* New York, 1941.

Lavignac, Albert. *Encyclopedie de la Musique.* 11 vols. Paris, 1913–1931.

Loewenberg, Alfred. *Annals of Opera, 1597–1940.* 2nd ed., rev. 2 vols. Geneva, 1955.

Martens, Frederick H. *A Thousand and One Nights of Opera.* New York, 1926.

McSpadden, Joseph W. *Light Opera and Musical Comedies.* New York, 1936.

Moser, Hans J. *Musik Lexikon.* 2 vols. Berlin, 1935.

Music Index. Detroit, 1949–date.

Musician's Guide. 3 vols. New York, 1954–1957.

National Association of Schools of Music. *List of Books on Music.* N.p., 1935.

New Oxford History of Music. London, 1954–. (In progress.)

Oxford History of Music. 2nd ed. Oxford, 1929–. (In progress.)

Pratt, Waldo Selden. *The New Encyclopedia of Music and Musicians.* New ed. New York, 1929.

Reese, Gustave. *Music in Renaissance.* Rev. ed. New York, 1959.

—————. *Music in the Middle Ages.* New York, 1940.

Repertoire International des Sources Musicales. Munchen, 1960–1961.

Riemann, Hugo. *Hugo Riemanns Musik Lexikon,* ed. Alfred Einstein. 2 vols. Berlin, 1929.

—————. *Opern-Handbuch.* Leipzig, 1881–1886.

—————. *Riemann Musik Lexikon.* 12 vols. New York, 1959–1961.

Sachs, Curt. *History of Musical Instruments.* New York, 1940.

Scholes, Percy A. *The Oxford Companion to Music.* 7th ed. London, 1947.

—————. *The Oxford Companion to Music.* 9th ed. London, 1955.

Slonimsky, Nicolas. *Music Since 1900.* 3rd ed. New York, 1949.

Smith, William James. *A Dictionary of Musical Terms in Four Languages.* London, 1961.

Strunk, William O. *State and Resources of Musicology in the United States.* American Council of Learned Societies. Washington Council, 1932.

Thompson, Oscar. *International Cyclopedia of Music and Musicians*, rev. Robert Sabin. 9th ed., rev. and enl. New York, 1964.

——————. *Plots of the Operas.* New York, 1940.

U.S. Library of Congress. Division of Music. *Catalogue of Opera Librettos Printed Before 1800*, ed. O. G. T. Sonneck. 2 vols. Washington, D.C., 1914.

Vannes, René. *Dictionnaire des Musiciens (Compositeurs).* Bruxelles, 1947.

——————. *Essai de Terminologie Musicale.* Thann, 1925.

Westrup, Jack A., and F. L. Harrison. *The New College Encyclopedia of Music.* New York, 1960.

Journals

ACTA Musicologia (ACTA Mus.)
American Music Teacher (Am. Mus. Tcr.)
Brass Quarterly (Brass Q.)
British Catalogue of Music (Brit. Cat. Mus.)
Clavier
Educational Music Magazine (Ed. Mus. Mag.)
Journal of Music Theory (J Mus. Theory)
Journal of Music Therapy (J. Mus. Therapy)
Journal of Renaissance and Baroque Music (J. Ren. & Baroq. Mus.)
Journal of Research in Music Education (J. Res. Mus. Ed.)
Journal of the American Musicological Society (J. Am. Mus. Soc.)
Modern Music (Modern Mus.)
Music and Letters (Mus. & Let.)
Music Index (Mus. Index)
Music Journal (Mus. J.)
Music Journal Biographical Cards
Musica Disciplina (Mus. Disc.)
Musical America (Mus. Am.)
Musical Quarterly (Mus. Q.)
Musical Record (Mus. R.)
Musical Times (Mus. T.)
Musician
Notes
Opera News (Opera N.)
Piano Teacher (Piano Tcr.)
Sonorum Speculum (Son. Spec.)
Tijdschrift Van De Vereniging voor Nederlandse Muziek G.

Philosophy

Books

Baldwin, James Mark. *Dictionary of Philosophy and Psychology.* 4 vols. New York, 1940–1949.

Bibliography of Philosophy, 1933–1936. New York, 1934–1937.

Hill, Johnson D., and W. R. Stuermann. *Philosophy and the American Heritage.* New York, 1961.

Miller, Hugh. *An Historical Introduction to Modern Philosophy.* New York, 1947.

Rand, Benjamin, comp. *Bibliography of Philosophy, Psychology and Cognate Subjects.* 2 vols. New York, 1905.

Runes, Dagobert D., ed. *The Dictionary of Philosophy.* New York, 1942.

Russell, Bertrand. *A History of Western Philosophy.* New York, 1945.

Schneider, Herbert W. *A History of American Philosophy.* 2nd ed. New York, 1963.

Urmson, J. O., ed. *The Concise Encyclopedia of Western Philosophy and Philosophers.* New York, 1960.

U.S. Library of Congress. Reference Department. *Philosophical Periodicals: An Annotated World List.* Washington, D. C., 1952.

Journals

American Philosophical Society, Proceedings (Proc. Am. Philos. Soc.)
Bibliography of Philosophy
Ethics
International Journal of Ethics (Int. J. Ethics)
Journal of Philosophy (J. Philos.)
Journal of Philosophy, Psychology, and Scientific Method (J. Philos., Psychol., & Sci. Method)
Journal of Symbolic Logic (J. Symbol. Logic)
Journal of the History of Ideas (J. Hist. Ideas)
Pacific Philosophy Forum
Personalist
Philosophia Mathematica (Philos. Math.)
Philosophical Review (Philos. Rev.)
Philosophy and Phenomenological Research (Philos. & Phenomenol. Res.)
Self Realization Magazine
Soviet Studies in Philosophy (Soviet Stud. Philos.)
Studies in Soviet Thought (Stud. Soviet Thought)

Psychology

Books

American Psychological Association. *Psy-*

Chological Abstracts Lancaster, Pa., 1927–date.

Monthly.

Annual Review of Psychology. Stanford, Calif., 1950–date.

Buros, Oscar K., ed. *Mental Measurements Yearbook.* 6th ed. New Brunswick, N. J., 1965.

Does not repeat information from edition to edition.

Chandler, Albert R., and E. N. Barnhart. *A Bibliography of Psychological and Experimental Aesthetics, 1864–1937.* Berkeley, Calif., 1938.

Divided into subject fields; lists books and journals from 1865–1937.

English, Horace B., and Ava C. English. *A Comprehensive Dictionary of Psychological and Psychoanalytical Terms.* New York, 1965.

Good, Carter V., and Douglas E. Scates. *Methods of Research: Educational, Psychological, Sociological.* New York, 1954.

Gowan, John Curtis, comp. *Annotated Bibliography on Creativity and Giftedness.* Northridge, Calif., 1965.

Grinstein, Alexander. *The Index of Psychoanalytic Writings.* 5 vols. New York, 1956–1960.

Handbook of Experimental Psychology. New York, 1951.

Harriman, Philip L., ed. *Encyclopedia of Psychology.* New York, 1946.

Harvard University. *The Harvard List of Books in Psychology.* Cambridge, Mass., 1949. Supplement, 1958.

Kiell, Norman. *Psychiatry and Psychology in the Visual Arts and Aesthetics: A Bibliography.* Madison, Wis., 1965.

Louttit, C. M. *Handbook of Psychological Literature.* Bloomington, Ind., 1932.

Mental Health Book Review Index. 1956–date.

Semi-annual.

Murchison, C. A., ed. *Handbook of Social Psychology.* 2 vols. Cambridge, Mass., 1954.

Psychological Index. 42 vols. 1894–1935.

Superseded by *Psychological Abstracts.*

Journals

American Journal of Psychology
American Journal of Psychotherapy
American Psychologist
Annual Review of Psychology
Behavioral Science
Child Development Abstracts and Bibliography

Contemporary Psychology
Journal of Abnormal & Social Psychology
Journal of Applied Behavioral Science
Journal of Applied Psychology
Journal of Clinical Psychology
Journal of Educational Psychology
Journal of Experimental Psychology
Journal of General Psychology
Journal of Individual Psychology
Journal of Psychology
Journal of Social Psychology
Menninger Quarterly
Psychological Abstracts
Psychological Bulletin
Psychological Monographs
Psychological Record
Psychological Review

Religion

Books

American Theological Association. *Index to Religious Periodical Literature: An Author and Subject Index to Periodical Literature, Including an Author Index to Book Reviews.* Chicago, 1949–1952–date.

Attwater, Donald, ed. *The Catholic Encyclopaedic Dictionary.* London, 1931.

Barrow, John Graves. *A Bibliography of Bibliographies in Religion.* Austin, Texas, 1955.

Butler, Alban. *Lives of the Saints,* ed. Herbert Thurston and Donald Attwater. Complete ed. 4 vols. New York, 1956.

Buttrick, George A., et al. *The Interpreter's Bible.* 12 vols. New York, 1951–1957.

————. *The Interpreter's Dictionary of the Bible.* New York, 1962.

Case, Shirley J., ed. *A Bibliographical Guide to the History of Christianity.* Chicago, 1931.

The Catholic Encyclopedia: An International Work of Reference on the Constitution, Doctrine, Discipline, and History of the Catholic Church. 16 vols. New York, 1913. Supplement, 1922.

The Catholic Periodical Index: A Guide to Catholic Magazines. Scranton, Pa., 1930–date.

Coulson, John, ed. *The Saints: A Concise Biographical Dictionary.* London, 1958.

Cross, F. L., ed. *The Oxford Dictionary of the Christian Church.* London, 1957.

Crow, Paul A., Jr. *The Ecumenical Movement in Bibliographical Outline.* New York, 1965.

Ferm, Vergilius T. A., ed. *An Encyclopedia of Religion.* New York, 1945.

Frazer, Sir James George. *The New Golden Bough,* ed. Theodor H. Gaster. New York, 1959.

Gibb, H. A. R., and J. H. Kramers, eds. *Shorter Encyclopaedia of Islam.* Leiden, 1953.

Hastings, James, ed. *Dictionary of the Bible,* rev. Frederick C. Grant. 5 vols. New York, 1963.

————. *Encyclopaedia of Religion and Ethics.* 7 vols. New York, 1951.

Illustrated World of the Bible Library, ed. Benjamin Mazar, Michael Avi-Yonah et al. New York, 1961.

International Association for the Study of History of Religions. *International Bibliography of the History of Religions, 1952–.* Leiden, Netherlands, 1952–date.

Joy, Charles R., comp. *Harper's Topical Concordance.* Rev. ed. New York, 1962.

Mayer, Frederick E., ed. *The Religious Bodies of America.* St. Louis, 1954.

Mead, Frank Spencer. *Handbook of Denominations in the United States.* 2nd rev. ed. New York, 1961.

Meissner, William W. *Annotated Bibliography in Religion and Psychology.* New York, 1961.

Miller, Madeleine S., and J. Lane Miller. *Harper's Bible Dictionary.* New York, 1952.

Morris, Raymond P. *A Theological Book List.* Naperville, Ill., 1960.

Nelson's Complete Concordance of the Revised Standard Version of the Bible, comp. John W. Ellison. New York, 1957.

Oxford Bible Atlas, ed. Herbert G. May, R. W. Hamilton, and G. N. S. Hunt. London, 1962.

Roth, Cecil, ed. *The Standard Jewish Encyclopedia.* Rev. ed. New York, 1962.

Schaff, Philip. *The New Schaff-Herzog Encyclopedia of Religious Knowledge,* ed. Samuel Jackson et al. New York, 1908–1912.

Smith, James Ward, and A. Leland Jamison, eds. *Religion in American Life.* Princeton, N. J., 1961–. (In progress.)

Strong, James. *The Exhaustive Concordance of the Bible.* New York, 1890.

Thompson, Newton W., and Raymond Stock. *Complete Concordance to the Bible* (Douay Version). St. Louis, 1945.

Union Theological Seminary. *A Basic Bibliography for Ministers.* 2nd ed. New York, 1960.

The Universal Jewish Encyclopedia. 10 vols. New York, 1939–1944.

Wright, George E., and Floyd V. Filson, eds. *The Westminster Historical Atlas to the Bible.* Rev. ed. Philadelphia, 1956.

Yearbook of American Churches. New York, 1915–date.

Zaehner, Robert C., ed. *The Concise Encyclopedia of Living Faiths.* London, 1959.

Journals

America
American Judaism (Am. Judaism)
The Biblical Archaeologist
Catholic Digest (Cath. Dig.)
Christian Century
Christian Herald
Christian Scholar
Christianity and Crisis
Church History (Church Hist.)
Commentary
Commonweal
Cross Currents
Dialog
Ecumenical Review (Ecumenical Rev.)
Ecumenist
Encounter
The Expository Times
Hibbert Journal
History of Religions (Hist. Relig.)
International Journal of Religious Education (Int. J. Relig. Ed.)
International Review of Missions (Int. Rev. Missions)
Interpretation: A Journal of Bible and Theology (Interpretation)
Journal for the Scientific Study of Religion (J. Sci. Study Relig.)
Journal of Religion (J. Relig.)
Motive
Religion in Life (Relig. in Life)
Religious and Theological Abstracts (Relig. & Theolog. Abstr.)
Religious Education (Religious Ed.)
Risk

Social Sciences

GENERAL
Books

Basler, Roy P., et al. *A Guide to the Study of the United States of America.* Washington, D.C., 1960.

Bellamy, Raymond F. *Preface to the Social Sciences.* New York, 1956.

Boyd, Anne M., and R. E. Rips. *United*

States Government Publications. 3rd ed. New York, 1950.

Chambers's World Survey. London, 1960– date.

Clarke, Jack A., ed. *Research Materials in the Social Sciences.* Madison, Wis., 1959.

Cohen, Benjamin A., ed. *The Worldmark Encyclopedia of the Nations.* New York, 1960.

Commager, Henry S., and Richard B. Morris, eds. *The New American Nation Series.* New York, 1954–. (In progress.)

Hoselitz, Berthold F., ed. *A Reader's Guide to the Social Sciences.* Glencoe, Ill., 1959.

New York State Library. *Checklist of Books and Pamphlets in the Social Sciences.* Albany, 1956–date.

Schmeckebier, Laurence F., and Roy B. Eastin. *Government Publications and Their Use.* Rev. ed. Washington, D.C., 1961.

Seligman, Edwin R. A., and Alvin Johnson. *Encyclopaedia of the Social Sciences.* 15 vols. New York, 1930–1935.

Tompkins, Dorothy C. *Methodology of Social Science Research: A Bibliography.* Berkeley, Calif., 1936.

United Nations Statistical Yearbook. Lake Success, N.Y., 1948–date.

U.S. Library of Congress. Exchange and Gift Division. *Monthly Checklist of State Publications.* Washington, D.C., 1910–date.

U.S. Superintendent of Documents. *Monthly Catalog of United States Government Publications.* Washington, D.C., 1895–date.

White, Carl M., et al. *Sources of Information in the Social Sciences: An Annotated Bibliography.* New York, 1959.

Zadrozny, John T., ed. *Dictionary of Social Science.* Washington, D.C., 1959.

ECONOMICS
Books

Batson, Harold Edward, comp. *A Select Bibliography of Modern Economic Theory, 1870–1929.* London, 1930.

Commodity Year Book. New York, 1939– date.

Dorfman, Joseph. *The Economic Mind in American Civilization.* 5 vols. New York, 1946–1959.

The Economic Almanac. New York, 1940– date.

Horton, Byrne, ed. *Dictionary of Labor Economics.* Washington, D.C., 1948.

——————. *Dictionary of Modern Economics.* Washington, D.C., 1948.

International Bibliography of Economics. Paris, 1952–date.

Palgrave, Sir Robert Harry Inglis. *Palgrave's Dictionary of Political Economy,* ed. Henry Higgs. 3 vols. London, 1925– 1926.

Public Affairs Information Service. New York, 1915–date.

Sloan, Harold S., and Arnold J. Zurcher, eds. *Dictionary of Economics.* 4th rev. ed. New York, 1961.

United Nations Bureau of Economic Affairs. *World Economic Survey.* New York, 1945–1947–date.

U.S. Bureau of Foreign and Domestic Commerce. *Foreign Commerce Yearbook.* 10 vols. Washington, D.C., 1934– 1951.

Winton, John R., ed. *Dictionary of Economic Terms.* 3rd rev. ed. London, 1951.

Woytinsky, W. S., and E. S. Woytinsky, eds. *World Population and Production: Trends and Outlook.* New York, 1953.

Journals

American Economic Review (Am. Econ. R.)
American Journal of Economics and Sociology (Am. J. Econ.)
Economic Bulletin (Econ. Bul.)
Economic Journal (Econ. J.)
Economic News (Econ. N.)
Economic Studies (Econ. Stud.)
Journal of Economic Abstracts (J. Econ. Abstr.)
Journal of Political Economy (J. Pol. Econ.)
Quarterly Journal of Economics (Q. J. Econ.)
Review of Economics and Statistics (Rev. Econ. & Statis.)
Southern Economic Journal (So. Econ. J.)

GEOGRAPHY
Books

American Geographical Society of New York. *Current Geographical Publications: Additions to the Research Catalogue of the American Geographical Society.* New York, 1938–date.

Cox, Edward Godfrey. *A Reference Guide to the Literature of Travel, Including Voyages, Geographical Descriptions, Adventures, Shipwrecks and Expeditions.* Seattle, Wash., 1935–1949.

James, Preston E., and Clarence F. Jones, eds. *American Geography: Inventory & Prospect.* Syracuse, N.Y., 1954.

Sealock, Richard B., and Pauline A. Seely. *Bibliography of Place Name Literature: United States, Canada, Alaska and Newfoundland.* Chicago, 1948.

Wright, John Kirtland, and Elizabeth T. Platt. *Aids to Geographical Research: Bibliographies, Periodicals, Atlases, Gazetteers and Other Reference Books.* 2nd ed. compl. rev. New York, 1947.

Journals
Annals of the Association of American Geographers (Assn. Am. Geog. Ann.)
Current Geographical Publications
Economic Geography (Econ. Geog.)
Geographical Review (Geog. R.)
Journal of Geography (J. Geog.)

HISTORY

Books
Adams, James Truslow, et al. *Album of American History.* 6 vols. New York, 1944–1953.
—————. *Dictionary of American History.* 2nd rev. ed. 6 vols. New York, 1942–1961.
American Historical Association. *Guide to Historical Literature,* ed. George F. Howe et al. New York, 1961.
Beers, Henry P. *Bibliographies in American History: Guide to Materials for Research.* Rev. ed. New York, 1942.
Bellot, Hugh H. *American History and American Historians: A Review of Recent Contributions to the Interpretation of the History of the United States.* Norman, Okla., 1952.
Bury, J. B., et al. *The Cambridge Ancient History.* 12 vols. Cambridge, 1923–1939.
Coulter, Edith M., and Melanie Gerstenfeld. *Historical Bibliographies: A Systematic and Annotated Guide.* Berkeley, Calif., 1935.
Current, Richard N., T. H. Williams, and Frank Freidel. *American History: A Survey.* New York, 1961.
Dutcher, George M., et al. *Guide to Historical Literature.* New York, 1931.
Gray, Wood. *Historian's Handbook: A Key to the Study and Writing of History.* Boston, 1959.
Gwatkin, Henry M., et al. *The Cambridge Medieval History.* 8 vols. Cambridge, 1911–1936.
Handlin, Oscar, et al. *Harvard Guide to American History.* Cambridge, Mass., 1954.
International Bibliography of Historical Sciences. Paris, 1926–date.
Langer, William L., ed. *An Encyclopaedia of World History.* Rev. ed. Boston, 1952.
Morris, Richard B., ed. *Encyclopedia of American History.* Rev. enl. ed. New York, 1961.

Pargellis, Stanley, and D. J. Medley, eds. *Bibliography of British History: The Eighteenth Century, 1714–1789.* Oxford, 1951.
Sarton, George. *Introduction to the History of Science.* Baltimore, 1927.
Schlesinger, Arthur M., and Dixon R. Fox, eds. *A History of American Life.* 13 vols. New York, 1927–. (In progress.)
Ward, A. W., et al. *The Cambridge Modern History.* 13 vols. Cambridge, 1902–1911.
Winsor, Justin, ed. *Narrative and Critical History of America.* 8 vols. Boston, 1884–1889.
Woodcock, Percival G., ed. *Concise Dictionary of Ancient History.* New York, 1955.
Writings on American History. Washington, D.C., 1902–1940.

Journals
American Historical Review (Am. Hist. Rev.)
Economic History Review (Econ. Hist. R.)
English Historical Review (Engl. Hist. R.)
Hispanic American Historical Review (Hispan. Am. Hist. R.)
History
History Today (Hist. Today)
Journal of American History (J. Am. Hist.)
Journal of Economic History (J. Econ. Hist.)
Journal of Modern History (J. Mod. Hist.)
Journal of Southern History (J. So. Hist.)
Journal of the History of Ideas (J. Hist. Ideas)
Past and Present
Renaissance News
Social Studies
Speculum

POLITICAL SCIENCE

Books
Adams, T. R. *Elements of Government: An Introduction to Political Science.* New York, 1960.
Beer, Samuel H., and Adam B. Ulam. *Patterns of Government: The Major Political Systems of Europe.* 2nd ed. New York, 1962.
Burchfield, Laverne. *Student's Guide to Materials in Political Science.* New York, 1935.
Documents on American Foreign Relations. Boston, 1939–date.
Hitchner, Dell Gillette, and William H. Harbold. *Modern Government: A Survey of Political Science.* 2nd ed. New York, 1965.
McLaughlin, Andrew C., and Albert B. Hart, eds. *Cyclopedia of American Government.* 3 vols. New York, 1914.

Palgrave, Sir Robert Harry Inglis. *Palgrave's Dictionary of Political Economy*, ed. Henry Higgs. 3 vols. London, 1925–1926.

Plano, Jack C., and Milton Greenberg. *The American Political Dictionary*. New York, 1962.

Political Handbook and Atlas of the World. New York, 1927–date.

Smith, Edward C., and Arnold J. Zurcher, eds. *New Dictionary of American Politics*. Rev. ed. New York, 1955.

The Statesman's Year-Book. London, 1864–date.

Theimer, Walter. *Encyclopedia of Modern World Politics*. New York, 1950.

Tompkins, Dorothy C. *Materials for the Study of Federal Government*. Chicago, 1948.

United Nations Yearbook. New York, 1947–date.

The Year Book of World Affairs. New York, 1947–date.

Journals

American Political Science Review (Am. Pol. Sci. R.)

Annals of the American Academy of Political and Social Science (Ann. Am. Acad. Pol. & Soc. Sci.)

Congressional Digest

Congressional Quarterly Almanac

Congressional Quarterly Weekly Report

Congressional Record

Current History

Foreign Affairs

Journal of Conflict Resolution (J. Conflict Resol.)

Journal of Politics (J. Pol.)

Midwest Journal of Political Science (Midwest J. Pol. Sci.)

Political Science Quarterly (Pol. Sci. Q.)

Public Administration Review (Pub. Adm. R.)

Public Opinion Quarterly (Pub. Opinion Q.)

Western Political Quarterly (West. Pol. Q.)

World Politics (World Pol.)

SOCIOLOGY

Books

Fairchild, Henry Pratt, ed. *Dictionary of Sociology*. New York, 1944.

Hastings, James, ed. *Encyclopaedia of Religion and Ethics*. 2nd ed. 7 vols. New York, 1951.

Reuter, Edward B. *Handbook of Sociology*. New York, 1941.

Seligman, Edwin R. A., ed. *Encyclopaedia of the Social Sciences*. 15 vols. New York, 1930–1935.

Social Work Year Book. New York, 1929–date.

U.S. Information Service. *Sociology and Social Work in the United States: A Bibliography*. Washington, D.C., 1959.

Journals

American Journal of Sociology (Am. J. Sociol.)

American Sociological Review (Am. Sociol. R.)

British Journal of Sociology (Brit. J. Sociol.)

Human Organization (Human Organ.)

International Social Science Journal (Int. Soc. Sci. J.)

Journal of Educational Sociology (J. Ed. Sociol.)

Journal of Marriage and the Family (J. Marriage & Fam.)

Social Education (Social Ed.)

Social Science (Social Sci.)

Social Science Abstracts (Social Sci. Abstr.)

Social Science Review (Social Sci. Rev.)

Sociological Abstracts (Social. Abstr.)

Sociological Quarterly (Sociol. Q.)

Sociology and Social Research (Sociol. & Soc. Res.)

Sociology of Education (Sociol. Ed.)

Speech and Drama

Books

American Educational Theatre Association. *A Bibliography of Theatre Arts Publications in English, 1963*, ed. Bernard F. Dukore. Evanston, Ill., 1965.

——————. *A Selected Bibliography and Critical Comment on the Art, Theory, and Technique of Acting*. Ann Arbor, Mich., 1948.

Baker, Blanch M., comp. *Dramatic Bibliography: An Annotated List of Books on the History and Criticism of the Drama and Stage and on the Allied Arts of the Theatre*. New York, 1933.

——————. *Theatre and Allied Arts: A Guide to Books Dealing with the History, Criticism, and Technic of the Drama and Theatre, and Related Arts and Crafts*. New York, 1952.

Belknap, Sara. *Guide to Dance Periodicals, 1941–*. New York, 1960–date.

——————. *Guide to the Performing Arts*. New York, 1957–date.

Blum, Eleanor. *Reference Books in the Mass Media: An Annotated, Selected Booklist Covering Book Publishing, Broadcasting, Films, Newspapers, Magazines, and Advertising*. Urbana, Ill., 1962.

Brigance, William Norwood, ed. *A History and Criticism of American Public Address.* 2 vols. New York, 1943.

Broderick, Gertrude G. *Radio and Television Bibliography.* Washington, D.C., 1956.

Chujoy, Anatole, ed. *The Dance Encyclopedia.* New York, 1949.

Cohen, Selma J., ed. *Dictionary of Modern Ballet.* New York, 1959.

Cumulated Dramatic Index, 1909–1949: A Cumulation of the F. W. Faxon Company's Dramatic Index. 2 vols. Boston, 1965.

The Dramatic Index for 1909–1949: Covering Articles and Illustrations Concerning the Stage and Its Players in the Periodicals of America and England and Including the Dramatic Books of the Year. 42 vols. Boston, 1910–1918; 1919–1952.

Duker, Sam. *Listening Bibliography.* New York, 1964.

Ewen, David. *Complete Book of the American Musical Theater: A Guide to More Than 300 Productions . . . From 1866 to the Present. . . .* New York, 1958.

————. *Encyclopedia of the Opera.* New York, 1955.

Fidell, Estelle A., and D. M. Peake, eds. *Play Index, 1953–1960: An Index to 4592 Plays in 1735 Volumes.* New York, 1963.

Firkins, Ina T. E., comp. *Index to Plays, 1800–1926.* New York, 1927. Supplement, 1935.

Fulton, A. R. *Motion Pictures: The Development of an Art from Silent Films to the Age of Television.* Norman, Okla., 1960.

Golter, Bob J. *Bibliography of Theses and Dissertations Relating to Audio-Visuals and Broadcasting.* Nashville, 1958.

Haberman, Frederick W., and James W. Cleary, comps. *Rhetoric and Public Address: A Bibliography: 1947–1961.* Madison, Wisc., 1964.

Harbage, Alfred. *Annals of English Drama, 975–1700: An Analytical Record of All Plays, Extant or Lost, Chronologically Arranged and Indexed by Authors, Titles, Dramatic Companies, Etc.* Rev. ed. Philadelphia, 1964.

Hare, Paul A. *Handbook of Small Group Research.* New York, 1962.

Hartnoll, Phyllis. *The Oxford Companion to the Theatre.* 2nd ed. London, 1957.

Hiler, Hilaire, and Meyer Hiler, comps. *Bibliography of Costume: A Dictionary Catalog of About Eight Thousand Books and Periodicals.* New York, 1939.

Hochmuth, Marie K., ed. *A History and Criticism of American Public Address.* Vol. III. New York, 1955.

International Federation of Library Associations. *Performing Arts Collections: An International Handbook.* Paris, 1960.

Lasswell, Harold D., Ralph D. Casey, and Bruce Lannes Smith. *Propaganda and Promotional Activities: An Annotated Bibliography.* Minneapolis, 1935.

Logasa, Hannah, comp. *An Index to One-Act Plays, 1900–1924.* Boston, 1924. Supplements, 1932–date.

Lowenberg, Alfred, comp. *The Theatre of the British Isles, Excluding London: A Bibliography.* London, 1950.

Mulgrave, Dorothy, et al. *Bibliography of Speech and Allied Areas, 1950–1960.* Philadelphia, 1962.

Nicoll, Allardyce. *A History of English Drama, 1660–1900.* Rev. ed. 6 vols. Cambridge, 1952–1959.

Ottemiller, John H. *Index to Plays in Collections: An Author and Title Index to Plays Appearing in Collections Published Between 1900 and 1962.* 4th ed. New York, 1964.

Rose, Oscar. *Radio Broadcasting and Television.* New York, 1947.

Siepmann, Charles Arthur. *Television and Education in the United States.* Paris, 1952.

Smith, Bruce L., and Chitra M. Smith. *International Communication and Political Opinion: A Guide to the Literature.* Princeton, N.J., 1956.

————, Harold D. Lasswell, and Ralph D. Casey. *Propaganda, Communication, and Public Opinion: A Comprehensive Reference Guide.* Princeton, N.J., 1946.

Stratman, Carl J. *Bibliography of Medieval Drama.* Berkeley, Calif., 1954.

Summers, Montague. *A Bibliography of the Restoration Drama.* London, 1934.

Thonssen, Lester, and Elizabeth Fatherson. *Bibliography of Speech Education.* New York, 1939. Supplement, 1950.

U.S. Office of Education. *Radio and Television: A Selected Bibliography.* Washington, D.C., 1960.

Van Lennep, William, et al. *The London Stage, 1660–1800: A Calendar of Plays, Entertainments & Afterpieces, Together With Casts, Box-Receipts and Contemporary Comment. Compiled from the Playbills, Newspapers and Theatrical Diaries of the Period.* Carbondale, Ill., 1960–. (In progress.)

Wallace, Karl R., ed. *History of Speech Education in America.* New York, 1954.

Welker, David, ed. *Ten Year Index of the Educational Theatre Journal: 1949–1958.* East Lansing, Mich., 1959.

West, Dorothy Herbert, and Dorothy Margaret Peake, comps. *Play Index, 1949 – 1952: An Index to 2616 Plays in 1138 Volumes.* New York, 1953.

Zettl, Herbert. *Television Production Handbook.* San Francisco, 1961.

Journals

Audio-Visual Communication Review (A-V Communication Rev.)

Business Screen (Bsns. Screen)

Educational Theatre Journal (Ed. Theatre J.)

Film News (Film N.)

Film Quarterly (Film Q.)

Modern Drama (Mod. Drama)

New York Guide and Theatre Magazine (NY Guide & Theatre Mag.)

New York Theatre Critics' Reviews (NY Theatre Critics' Rev.)

Quarterly Journal of Speech (Q. J. Speech)

Radio and Television News (Radio & TV N.)

Speech Monographs (Speech Mon.)

The Speech Teacher (Speech Teach.)

Studies in Public Communication (Stud. Public Communication)

Television Magazine (TV Mag.)

Television Quarterly (TV Q.)

Theatre

Theatre Arts

Theatre Arts Monthly

Tulane Drama Review (Tulane Drama R.)

INDEX

2 3 4 5 6 7 8 9 10 11 12 13 14 15 16 17 18 19 20 21 22 23 24 25   SH   74 73 72 71 70 69 68